REPLY '

A collection of ridiculous time-wasting chats with scammers from around the globe.

BY STEVE HIGGINS

"Trampette du jour to you, dear reader. Welcome to my world of pushing fraudsters to the brink of insanity!"

When most of us get an unwanted email or message, the first thought is to click the delete button, but one man can't resist replying to all of them. These are Steve Higgins' ridiculous time-wasting chats with the desperate scammers trying to take his money.

Find out what happened when this serial time-waster won an unexpected fortune in an American lottery, how the Illuminati promised to make him all-powerful with a magic ring, and why a witchdoctor offered him an enchanted ointment to help with a little problem in the trouser department. Steve also proves that true love knows no bounds as romance blossoms, with exceptional ease, despite a lack of physical proximity. It seems love is on the cards for Steve and the ever-confused Russian temptress, Svetlana, even with the restrictions of his current living conditions.

Confused scammers from around the globe try to understand Steve's ludicrous use of near-English language and his fictitious topics of conversation, including such absurd events as Rosbeck Friday, a nationally recognised day where chalkboards are the preferred method of communication.

Steve also conspires with a secret society to avenge the death of his uncle, who was killed on a tiki island themed movie set by a huge falling fibreglass volcano; and corresponds with Dr. Hassan, an African love doctor who consults his oracle to find magical ways to bring a former lover back in to Steve's life and even guides him towards his goal of having his own little baby boy called Graham.

Join Steve on his journey to the magical temple of Kingsleekwebelem, as he confuses con artists, frustrates fraudsters and generally wastes the time of anyone who dares to contact him.

Inbox

1. From Russia With Lies
A surprise email from a Russian dating agency lands in my inbox with an introduction to Anna, a Russian singleton who is very keen to come and visit me in London.

2. The Laziest Fraudster Ever
A brief encounter with a lazy scammer who really needs to work on his defrauding scripts.

3. I Won The Lottery
A very patient lottery official named David Ray helped me collect the $350,000 owed to me, after an email informed me of a surprise win in an annual sweepstake.

4. For Better Or Worse
I learn all about the ever-confused Russian temptress, Sveta. Follow us as our relationship blossoms, despite the restrictions of my current living conditions.

5. Love In The Nick Of Time
'Time and relative dimension in space' proves to be an obstacle between me and the rotten gooseberry of my heart, Agnessa, but will love conquer all?

6. A Witchdoctor Helped Me Become A Real Man
When I was presented with a potential cure for my embarrassing personal inadequacy by a real African witchdoctor named Dr. Abaka, I jumped at the chance to become a bigger man, no matter what the cost.

7. Becoming All-Powerful With An Unforgettable Illuminati Finger Ring
After a close relative was killed on a tiki island themed movie set by a huge falling fibreglass volcano, a sub-master from an infamous secret society promised a way to avenge this senseless death.

8. An African Love Doctor Cured My Broken Relationship

Dr. Hassan consults his oracle to find magical ways to bring a former lover back in to my life and even guides me towards my goal of having my own little baby boy called Graham.

9. Black Balled By The Nigerian Branch Of The Illuminati

My dreams of becoming an Illuminati member are dashed when society member, James Barry, threatens to kill me and my family on the seventh day because I didn't take his sacred oath seriously.

10. The Illuminati Shopping List

Once again The Illuminati have invited me to join their prestigious group, but before I can attend my initiation ceremony at the temple in a place I'm told is called "Kingsleekwebelem," I need to buy some rather special items.

11. Resting Grinch Face

Cultural difficulties obstruct potential love and a tempting business deal put on the table over Christmas by Isabella, the new grumpy and humourless woman in my life.

From Russia With Lies

"Land of Love"
Greetings friend!!!

This letter arrived to you from Russian
Internet dating agency "Land of Love".
Our client miss Anna, 25 years old from
Saint Petersburg, Russia. She
addressed to our agency. She wants to
search man from USA for friendship or
love. Miss Anna is never married and
have no children. You can see miss
Anna at picture.

> This sounds great, Anna sounds
> perfect only I'm not American, I'm in
> the UK.
>
> Do you have anyone else on your
> books who might be suitable?
>
> Steve

My name is Anna. My birthday on April,
20th 1983. And me 26 years will be
fast. I live in Russia, in very beautiful
city of St.-Petersburg. I very cheerful
and beautiful woman. And I wish to be
even happier. I live and I work in Russia
as the children's teacher.

As you already understand to write to
you my first letter I have addressed in
agency of acquaintances. I have paid
there 7 dollars, and to me have told
that my letter will be sent to lonely to

the man which wishes to meet the woman from Russia.

I as very much hope that you like my photos, and you would like to meet me. I am valid for a photo, and you can see me in the future.

The matter is that it is very fast, namely on March, 4th I can receive the visa to your country. Therefore I very much hope that we could have our meeting. I for the first time in the life shall visit the Europe, and I to not have friends or the friend in the Europe.

But also I have some questions for you:
1. Whether you can meet me on March, 5th?
2. What airport will be more convenient for our meeting?

Your friend from Russia Anna

Hi Anna,

I am always interested in meeting new people, however I'm not looking for a relationship right now.

But if you wanted someone to show you around London then I would be more than happy. The 5th March is my birthday but I'm not celebrating it until the weekend so I am free on the day.

I can get to Heathrow Airport in about 20 minutes from where I live if you wanted a tour guide.

Sorry, I don't have a photo on me at the moment as I am in work.

Steve

How are you doing? I hope that you well today and you have good day today and excellent mood. I am very happy to receive your letter and the nobility that you really wish our meeting, and you can meet me in the airport.

As I already spoke in this letter I would like to tell not much more about me. Therefore I write to you all that I think, and all that comes to my head. And though I understand, that one our meeting cannot replace hundred letters, I nevertheless shall write to you as much as possible about me and my life.

Mine mum and the daddy live separately 10 years. Now the daddy the pensioner, also lives one in the house in a wood, the daddy is engaged in hunting and fishing. Earlier my father worked as the dental doctor.

My mum call Oksana. I live with my mum in our house. Now my mum too the pensioner, but earlier mum worked at factory, mum murder will out clothes.

Yours Anna.

Hello,

I mostly don't understand what you are saying, but all sounds fine to me.

Just let me know your plans as they develop, perhaps I can help you with your English while you are here too.

Steve

I am happy to receive your letter very soon.
But I do not understand, what you to not understand in my letter?
And why you do not write to me about yourself?
Yours Anna.

Sorry, I just found your email quite hard to read, your English isn't too good. For example....

"Now the daddy the pensioner, also lives one in the house in a wood, the daddy is engaged in..."

The daddy? Do you mean "your Daddy" or "my Daddy" ..."the daddy" doesn't make sense.

"Now my mum too the pensioner, but earlier mum worked at factory, mum murder will out clothes."

I'm not sure what "my mum to the pensioner means", do you mean "my Mum is a pensioner" and "murder", she is a murderer?

And this, I didn't understand... "About that that now I shall fly to Belgium all my family knows and all are happy, that I can visit your country."

Sorry to be picky, I just struggled a bit and I'm now worried that language may be a barrier when we meet.

To tell you a bit about me... my name is Steve Bronce Higgins and I am twelvety-eight.

I have lived in London since October, I work in finance... not a god place to be right now. My parents both live in Oxford where I am from. My hobbies are walking, running and shoe restoration.

Steve
x

I understand that my English is not so good. My mum not the murderer, my mum makes clothes. My daddy the pensioner, and it lives now not with us. My parents have divorced 10 years ago.

I very cheerful and sports woman, I always went in for sports, and most of all I love aerobics. I am engaged in gymnastics, and dances. I when did not smoke, and I do not take alcohol, only in special cases. (the Birthday, New Year)

I as when was not married, and have no children. And now I have no what boyfriend. Therefore I am absolutely free. But I very much like to waste time with mine friends, my mum and the sister.

I very much like to go to a campaign, to go to a wood, in mountains....... It is fine. On fresh air I can spend all the day because I love fresh air. I very much like our nature. And in the house of my mother there are two horses, I love walk on horses.

It is a pity to me, that we cannot call each other, but my mobile phone is not included. I hope that you understand it?

Yours Anna.

Hi Anna,

Nice reading your email. Glad to hear you like the outdoors, me too!

You also said you like to go to a campaign in the woods and mountains? What campaigns do you mean?

I am pleased that you are looking forward to meeting up, how are your plans coming together? As I said in my first email though, I'm not interested in starting a romantic relationship but your friendship is welcome.

Steve
x

Hello my dear Steve!

I am very happy to receive your letter, I really hope that we can be greater friends.

I really very much like to have a rest in a wood and mountains. I to go from mountain with friends with whom I went to school.

Our company very amicable and we always have good time. And that you to do for rest.

I understand from your letter that you to search only friendship but why you do not want more serious attitudes?

Thanks once again for your emails, I am enjoying talking with you.

Well after the last relationship I was in I'm not sure about going in to another romantic partnership. To be honest with you, it all ended a bit badly last time. I'm still being dragged through the courts over all of that. It wasn't really my fault, I just got angry and she fell and landed in an awkward way.

I guess I am open to the possibility of romantic eggulisations but it would take me a little bit of time to get resdunded. We'll just have to see how well we get on I suppose, after all, you are very attractive.

So you like to walk in the woods? You don't take part in campaigns there?

Steve
x

Good morning my lovely Steve!

How are you today? I hope that all well and you to have good day today and good mood.

My work will come to an end yesterday, and I can study more Moscow, and in my letter I shall write to you more about this fine city.

Why you do not write to me more about the city???????? Your city is really beautiful? What is especially beautiful? When I shall arrive to you I very much would like to have walks of the pedestrian with you, I very much like to walk.

To walk on night city, to hold your hand and to look at stars.................. I really think that it very beautifully.

I very much ask you to write to me more how you understand love???? Whether you can grow fond of me???? You when loved on the present??? You had a love.

Kiss you.
Anna.

Good morning, I hope you are well!

The reason I tend not to write much is that I find your emails quite difficult to read and I am unsure how easily you are understanding my English. For example, your questions you have asked me to answer, I don't really understand them.

I very much ask you to write to me more how you understand love???? How I understand love? Do you mean, what does love mean to me?

Whether you can grow fond of me???? I may be able to grow fond of you, you are very beautiful in your photos and you seem very sweet.

You when loved on the present??? You had a love.
I don't know what this means - it doesn't make sense.

OK, I'll tell you more about London. I have been living here since October. My favourite places to go are the Science Museum which is really good fun and interesting. I like to walk but since I have moved here I haven't had much opportunity, I'm along way from countryside now. I do like to walk along the Thames at night though. Although there's not much chance of seeing the stars in London.

I work in Canary Wharf which is a really nice part of town, very modern and the home of several large banks. I live in Vauxhall in a big apartment block overlooking the Thames. Unfortunately I live on the wrong side of the building to get the best view.

Hope you have a good day, looking forward to seeing you... it's only a week today!!

Steve
x

Good day my lovely Steve!!!

I hope that you well feel very well this morning in this day.

I sad not much..................... But to sad only because we cannot already be together today. I really very much wish to be with you. I want that you held my hand and looking in my eyes, spoke me about our love.

I really hope that you to admire with my beauty, and I hope that you will be always happy that. I shall be near to you.

My heart is really compressed each time when I think of you. When I receive your letter.................... I think that I require you.

Each time I fly as a bee, I wish to arrive to you and this big happiness for me that you too to want it.

I very much hope that your words, and your desire sincere..................... Also that this Fairy tale, was a reality and we were in love.

Millions kisses for you and all my love.

For ever yours Anna.

P.S I ask to write you more what to feel your heart.

Oh my gosh, your emails really are becoming increasingly difficult to read.

Please could you answer a few of my questions....
1) Can you speak English or are you using a translator?
2) Do you think we will be able to talk OK when we meet?
3) Have you arranged somewhere to stay in London and how long are you staying?
4) Do you know what time your flight gets in to the city yet? Looking online it seems flights from Moscow land at 8, 8:50 and 9:30am.

I cannot talk more about the feeling from my heart, we have only been emailing for a few days. I am looking forward to meeting you and I think you are hot but I can't say I love you and couldn't describe our meeting as a fairytale as you have.

Meeting will be fun and exciting and if you are as beautiful in real life as you seem to be in your photos, and, as I have previously said, if your poor understanding of the English language doesn't stand in our way then our friendship could well develop in to something more serious.

Steve
x

Good morning my lovely Steve!

I each time am happy to receive your letter. But me sadly nobility that that my English language is not absolutely well clear for you. But I try to write each time all more clear for you.

1. I am really independent I can speak in English, and I do not use the translator.

2. I think that we can understand each other when we shall meet.

3. I for the present do not know where I shall remain in London.

4. On Monday I shall go to the airport and to reserve the ticket for me. I shall inform you details on Monday. Oк?

I as understand, that your heart still is not yet in love, and you to not feel yet what to feel my heart. But I very much hope that all will soon vary, and my letters will like your heart.

I kiss you also wait for your letter.
Yours Anna.

Hi,

I thanks, yeas well I am happy moods.

Let me give you a few pointers on your English if you don't mind...

You wrote:
"I each time am happy to receive your letter. But me sadly nobility that that my English language is not absolutely well clear for you"

This should be written:
"You make me happy each time I receive your email, but it saddens me that you find that my English language isn't absolutely clear"

I hope that helps and that I don't sound contraflabbed or dismeaning.

WOW, you're not booking your flight until Monday? Are you going to be able to book it at such short notice? Do you know what part of London you'll be staying in. I live in South-North London so just wondered if you would be near me.

I probably won't get a chance to email you again today as my company respect Rosbeck Friday when we cut ourselves off from email and internet communication and speaking to each other only through verbal methods (and of course chalk board).

Most of London practices Rosbeck Friday as it is one of the seven-twenty large capital business district in the upper Earth region. Lord Geoffrey Rosbeck first introduced the Internet-free day back in 1936, it increases productivity, creativity and of course productivity.

So, happy Rosbeck Friday to you, look forward to seeing you soon.

Steve
x

Good day my love............. My dream Steve!!!

I hope that this day passes well for you and you have good day and very good mood.

Today there was very sated day for me. I could see many beautiful places in Moscow because I was on excursion on Moscow, and heard about this city much.

I very much hope that we shall have greater love, and we can visit Moscow together and see this beautiful city, and I hope that we can see city in which I live.

Today when, I saw their beautiful persons, persons of enamoured people I was happy. It is happy because I dreamed about ours with you a meeting and I hope that as also we shall have our passionate kisses, and we shall be happy in the future.

I wish to do you happy because I think that you very good the man and you have deserved it.

Now I wish to learn you as the man more, and to tell about my character.

Yours Anna.

Moscow sounds almost as beautiful and amazing as you. I think they most interesting place I've visited is Rosham. It's a small farm near Brocknill but it's massive! I love it there, they have cows, they have pigs, they have sheep, they have turkeys, they have ducks, they have hens, they have horses, they have cows, they have children and they have budgies and they have queggs.

I know queggs aren't animals but they had a whole barn full of them, I took about 74.6 home with me, we were eating roast quegg for the next month, it was so funny that milk came out of my nose.

I was chatting to a friend about you at scholk today, I was telling him how excited I am that a hot Russia girl (you) is coming to visit me via the gift of airplane through the sky. We ended up having an argument, he says that you have cars in Russia but last time I was there I didn't see a single car any where. I bet him 5 daktar that there weren't cars. So, are there cars? I am right aren't I?

My days has been quite good so far, Rosbeck Friday is always a fun day. As I said earlier, we've been communicating in 1940s style all day today, I have chalk all over me and my pylons are pointy.

You want to know more about me as a man, my character? OK, well being bisexual I am very open minded, I am very spiritual, I believe in ghosts, rats and UFO (Unidentified Fried Omelets). I have seven hairs and strong beliefs in the occult.

When I was 8 I was trapped in a basement for 7 years, I think this is what lead to my claustrophobia and agoraphobia which I suffer from now. I was kept for 7 years by a manbearpig (basically it's someone who is half man, half bear and half pig - you are probably familiar with bears coming from Russia, I read that you have the biggest population of Yogi Bears in the world).

Since then I haven't been able to look a bear in the eyes, I don't trust them anymore. I think it was this experience which led to my, let's say, changeable moods. Luckily I haven't hurt anyone in some time so you should be fine.

I find it exciting in my pants the way that the more we talk to each other, the stronger my feelings become. This may sound silly as I realise that we have never met and that we've only been emailing for a week... but in time, I think I could really fall for you in the style of love.

Take care my sweet ambush,
Steve
x

Good morning for you my lovely Steve!

I understand that my English not so well, and you to laugh over me.................... It is amusing. But I when to not ignore your questions, and I certainly wish to answer all questions which you have for me but I cannot understand all that you write to me.

I walked today really much and had fine day. Today very warm and to walk pleasantly but every minute I thought of you and our meeting.

I think that our meeting can really do us very happy.

I kiss you also wait for your letter.
Yours Anna.

Sorry I didn't mean to laugh at you, let me explain... if you spent the day walking you would say "I spent the day walking". A "pedestrian" is a person who walks at the side of a road. When you combine words, the phrase "walks of the pedestrian" is actually quite rude, it's a euphemism for a quite dirty sexual act.

So to say you have been doing "walks of the pedestrian" would mean that you spent the day with two men... and well, let's leave it at that.

Only two days now until you book your flight, you must be very excited! I can't wait until Thursday! I've never met a Russian human before.

Steve
x

Good morning my lovely Steve!

I understand that you think of me much and that you want ours I shall meet. I as very much wish to be with you and I dream of you every minute. And how you have lead yesterday? What did you do yesterday?

I walked yesterday because Moscow really very beautiful city, and it is very pleasant to me to see Moscow really much.

As I already wrote, tomorrow I shall go to travel agency and I shall reserve my ticket. Therefore tomorrow in the morning I shall inform you time and date of flight.

I kiss you my love.

Forever yours Anna.

Good morning to you too my lovely beef cake!

I hope you are OK and have had a good day, mine has been fine. I've been attacking swans at John Craven Park, which is a big park in London - it's a great place to walk if you are mentally retarded.

I can't believe that you are booking your flight tomorrow, the week has gone by so quickly!!! I've very excited and looking forward to Thursday!!

Can I ask you, when we meet... I realise that I don't know you too well but when we meet will it be OK to touch you? May be even offer you the free gift of a hug? I have never hugged a lady before.

Let me know if you need any help with sorting out a hotel, of course I will be able to help you with luggage at the airport and provide you with a lift to your hotel to drop your things off, unless of course you would rather come straight back to my apartment for a look around ...or whatever.

Kisses to you too bradley,
Steve
xxx

Good morning my lovely Steve!

I hope that this week-end was fine for
you and you had good time and
excellent mood. I am very happy to
receive your letter, and to realize that
up to our meeting to remain all of less
time and already very soon I can
embrace you, and certainly kiss.

Today I shall go to travel agency and to
reserve the ticket for me. As soon as I
shall know more information on my
ticket, and all to a detail I shall write to
you the letter.

I really have very complex nights now
because every minute I think only of
you. I close eyes and I represent our
meeting. In our meeting all will be
beautifully and perfectly.

Now I should go.
Forever yours Anna.

P.S Please send me yours
foto .... I want see you.

Word up Anna my main man!

The weekend passed fine for me and
my mood is supreme. I am also hella
glad that out meeting to remain all of
less time, in just 5.8 days I will be able

to embrace your face open and may be even plant kisses on your eyes.

Great, I hope all goes well at the travel advisory board and that they are able to sort out your tickets, tickets, tickets!

I am looking forward with both my actual eyes to hearing how you got on, cough.

I hope your head is full of beauty today as you start to pack your dogs and owl parts in to your luxurious leather suitcase.

My nights are also very complex as I think of you more than seven times an hour.

I am in work right now at this very second moment so I don't have a photogiraffe that I can send but let me describe my self to you via words of typing. I am 9 foot 4 foot 6, I have four cream coloured eye and six hairs which are made of brown. My beard is not on my face and I have roughly two face-adjoined ears which I hear with.

What do you think? Like the sound of me? Think you will like me?

I will send on a photo later this evening when the fire ball weighs low in the sky.

Take care, see you in three days.

I am throwing love at you,
Steve
x

Hello my love, my the intimate friend Steve!!!
How are you???? I hope that you well today and your heart is full of happiness and love.
Now still Monday, and I understand that you already to require a detail of my flight, but please understand that I can to give all to a detail only on Wednesday when I shall receive my visa.
I dream about our first kiss, our embraces.

It's so good to hear from you, it seems like you are the type of girl who likes to leave things until the last minute.
So, you are getting your tickets on Wednesday, when do you intend to fly, Wednesday or Thursday?
I thought you would be flying on Wednesday evening so that you arrive early on Thursday morning so that we have the whole day together.
Do you know where you will be staying yet in London?
I'm so glad everything is OK between us again.
Steve
xxxx

Good morning my lovely Steve!!!
Today really there was very complex day for me because it was difficult to receive for me the visa.
Today after I have received the visa, I have hastened in travel agency, where I to reserve my ticket to pay it and to have the information.

But I could not make it. Problem in that I have the tourist visa. With this visa I should have the insurance document that I can be in your country independently.
That is I should have at me cashes.
And minimal quantity which I should have it 1500 dollars.
I do not know that to me to do now.
I have the visa, but I cannot pass customs.
Therefore I ask you. You could help me with this money???
I shall not spend it, I shall bear only it on customs and as soon as I to arrive to you in the airport, I shall give this money.
Millions kisses for you.
For ever yours Anna.

Hi Anna,
That is bad news about the visa, so you would only need to borrow the money for the next 24 hours or so? Don't you have any spending money at all???
Hmmm... I am unsure, is that Russian dollars? I've just had a look at the exchange rate, that's about £30 - I mean it's not a huge amount so I guess I could send it to you via PayPal or something.
May be you could just buy me a meal when you get here in exchange or something.
When do you need to get this sorted by?
Steve
x

I do not know as works PayPal.

Please simply go to the Western Union
and to send money there.
To me have told that it works very
quickly.
Only 15 minutes, and I can receive
money here.
I can receive money here in Russia in
15 minutes as soon as you will send
money.
Please to not worry about it
Anna.

This all sounds very complicated for
the insides of my head and my brain,
as it is just £30 could I not just use
PayPal? PayPal is an instant transfer.
I've never used Western Onion before
so I am not sure how this process
wonky-works.
Steve
x

Steve.
I not absolutely understand you. I shall
require in 1500 USA dollars.
You understand it?
You can send me 1500 dollars USA?
I should have this of money for
customs, and there is no other variant.
You have no 1500 US dollars?
I shall wait your help.
Millions kisses for you.
For ever yours Anna.

Oh! USA dollars? Sorry, that's why I
was confused... in the UK we use (£)
British Pounds (GBP) so I assumed you
must have meant 1500 Russian Rubles
which is £30 (GPB) British Pounds.

My lunch break is in 20 minutes and there is a Western Onion near by.
1,500.00 RUB = 29.4534 GBP so I'll send you £30.
I'll let you know as soon as it is done.
Steve
x

A LITTLE WHILE LATER...

Hi Anna,

It's all done so the money should be with you shortly, I made the transaction about half of 60 minutes ago so it should be ready for your sister to collectionate.
I think I need to give you the following details...

Sent in the name of: Stephen Elizabeth Higgins

My address: 41 Harleyford Rd, Vauxhall, London, SE11 5AY

The M.T.C.N. is: 9819584492

And I'm not sure if you need the reference: AKR9379AD

I hope that is all OK, one problem though. I sent £1070 but there was a charge, it was only £6.78 so I paid £1076.87 in total, will you be OK to cover that cost once you are here?

Salad love,
Steve
x

My love Steve!
My sister just has come back from the western Union.
And she could not receive money. Have told that probably you did not do translation.
Or has made a mistake in MTCN.
Whether please to check up correctly you has specified number.
Or can you send a scan me?

Oh my Irish god in Devon, I'm so sorry!!!!
The number is 9829584492.
I must have typed it incorrectly.
I can send a scan you but I don't have a scanner at work, I won't be home for another 3 Earth hours.
Steve

Steve,
You to not play with me because I just checked new number on a site of the Western Union and it too does not work.
The sister spoke with the Western Union, and there have told that they have no the information on that that you sent money.
You understand?

What?! Geoff God! I hope it hasn't gone missing somewhere! I knew I shouldn't have used Western Onion! I am unfamiliar with how they operate.
The MTCN number is as I said previously 9829584492, that's what it says on the receipt.

I trusted you and used Western Onion
with your advice, I hope you haven't
cost me money!
Steve

You to not deceive me? To my sister
have told that you did not send money.
You understand it?
Please to scan the receipt as soon as
possible and to send it to me.
Then we can probably receive money.
I think that you simply to deceive me
that you sent money, but did not do it.
You were in the Western Union today?
Yours Anna.

You have changed.... it seems like you
are only talking to me for my money!
Earlier today you were telling me you
loved me, now you are calling me a
liar!!
I am being as honest as you are.

I do not name you the liar.
And I all still love you but I to be
nervous that I all in the airport, and I do
not know as to fly.
You understand me?
But I love you, LOVE, LOVE, LOVE!

I don't like to hear that you are stuck in
an air carriage portal on your own, I am
also worried about the money what I
are sent.
I will send a scan of the receipt as soon
as I can.
I love you too, in a way.
Steve

OK' I will wait yours letter. I LOVE YOU!

I found a scanner on one of the floors
here, sub-level 165 and managed to
scan the receipt, see attached
attachment which I have attached.
I love you right through to the bottom
of your filthy black heart.
I hope that so we can get married soon
and I can do sex on you for many
hours. May be even some small sex
babies could pop out and we could
name them Fox and Mulder and then
punish and mock them for being too
young to even walk! Idiots, what kind
of humans can't walk!?!
See you tomorrow,
Love forever and sometimes,
Steve
x

Steve,
Good work..................... But you to
make a mistake.
You have lost the woman which have
really grown fond of you.

The Laziest Fraudster Ever

Hello you ready to recieve your atm
card?

> Great, thanks!

Can you come down here and get you
approval slip to sign. At the bank.

> Yeah sure, no problem. Where do I
> need to go?

Very good. Come to Nigeria. In the next
email give me your flight details.

I Won The Lottery

Attention: Winner
From: Mrs. Mariam Benson

You won the sum of $350,000.00 UNITED STATES DOLLARS from our yearly sweepstakes 2010. Your email address was among the five lucky winner in our computer email ballot. You are hereby advice to contact Mr. John Eddy to claim your prize (fpost88888@att.net).

CLAIMS PROCESSING REQUIREMENT DATA:
(1) Full Names: _____
(2) Sex: _____
(3) Age: _____
(4) Country:_____
(5) Mobile Phone: _____

Note: the only money you will send to Mr. John Eddy to deliver your Consignment direct to your postal Address in your country is just ($120 .00 USD) only being Security Keeping Fee of the Courier Company so far.

Sincerely,
Mrs. Mariam Benson.

THAT ALL SEEMED TO BE TOTALLY LEGITIMATE AND IN ORDER, SO I SENT MY DETAILS OVER AS QUICKLY AS I COULD.

Winning Lottery Claim
From: Steve Higgins

I had an email from Mariam Benson stating that I have won the lottery, what a great start to the year!!!

Here's the details required....
(1) Steve Higgins
(2) Male
(3) 30
(4) UK
(5) 07816 285931

You mentioned a postal fee of $120? Is that British or American dollars? How would I pay that and is there any other cheaper options such as a bank transfer of the winnings?

Thanks,
Steve

Make this payment today
From: David Ray

You are to make this payment today via WESTERN UNION OR MONEY GRAM OUTLET in the name of our accounting officer:
NAME: MR. JOHN NELSON.
ADDRESS: ABUJA NIGERIA
You are to forward payment information to us via this email after making the payment, the details are as follows:

SENDER'S
NAME:....................... ....
...
SENDER'S ADDRESS.................

AMOUNT SENT:
$120.................... ....
.....
TEXT QUESTION: in god?
TEXT ANSWER: .we trust
MONEY TRANSFER CONTROL
NUMBER
(M.T.C.N)......................................

Upon receipt of the above, modalities
to send your certificate and cheque will
commence immediately.
We want you to note that your parcel
will get to you in 1 (ONE) days after
your transfer has being confirmed.

Sincerely,
MR. DAVID RAY
FEDEX CONTROLLER, EXPRESS
COURIER COMPANY

British or US dollars?
From: Steve Higgins

Hi David,

Thanks for your email, I was just
speaking to one of your representatives
over the phone (he called me), he
seemed a little bit rude and ended the
call while I was trying to ask a question
- can you please check that it was
someone from your oganisation who
called me as it seemed a bit odd?

I needed to check whether the $120
was British or US dollars - as I live in
the UK but this is the US lottery. If you
can clear up this detail then I can make
the payment on the way home from
work today.

As the delivery will take 1 (one) day, would it be possible to get the delivery address changed to my work address as I won't be home much over the next couple of days.

Thanks,
Steve

"Network Problems"
From: David Ray

I hope this email get to you in good state of mind,

We are very sorry for the conversation on phone it was our network over here that is why we have that problem we are very sorry about that this is what you have to do I will be sending to you the payment instructions on how to make the payment true money gram and for the currency you can pay it in pounds and get back to us with the payment information from the bank very early.

Sincerely,
MR. DAVID RAY
FEDEX CONTROLLER, EXPRESS
COURIER COMPANY

Payment Sent
From: Steve Higgins

Hi there,
It's me again, Steve (Slim)... the good news is (well the good news is I won the lottery!!) but also, I managed to

make it in to my local branch of Money Gram on my way home from work yesterday,

I thought you were going to phone to obtain the required details from me last night so I waited by my phone for most of the evening but I failed to receive your call which is sad.

But any way, I have made the payment of £120 (UK) and have all the confirmation details for you when you are ready to take them.

Thanks again for all your help with this,
Steve (Higgins)

I await your response today
From: David Ray

Hello,

I called you yesterday and your sister and brother pick up the phone and I was very upset sins you have make the payment I want you to scan the payment slip from money gram to our email so that our account officer to confirm the payment so that we can get back to you with all the information to obtain your winning prize.

So I await your response today with all the payment details from money gram,

Thanks and God bless you,
Mr. David Ray

Owl Sorry

From: Steve Higgins

Hi Mr Rogers,

I'm owl so sorry about Jane and Martin, I think they may have taken my phone and replaced it with a "dummy phone" which I was unaware of - how annoying!! I'm sorry if this has slowed things down.

I'm very sorry for any incongrulance this may have caused and I hope it has affected the time in which I can claim my prize winning funds.

I have only just read your email (and I am now in work) so I don't (have) the Money Gram document with me but I will head home at lunch and bring them back to work with me, I will then scan them using our RICOH Africo MP C4500 PCL 5c prints/copier/scanner that we have here in the office and I will then at the highest speed our highspeed dedicated internet pipeline allows, email them direct to your inbox (fpost8@catt.net).

Thanks,
Steve

Proof of Payment
From: Steve Higgins

Hi Ray,

Attached is a scan of the document Money Gran gave me.
My postal address at my work office is:
Lackborn House,

Marley Way,
Teilve Industrial Estate,
Vauxhall
London
SW6 4BB

Thanks for all your help with this,
Mr Higgins

Payment On Hold
From: David Ray

Hello,

Your payment you make from the
Money Gram we did not pick it up by
our account officer because the money
was hold down by the Money Gram
you make the payment.

This is what you have to do you have to
go to the money gram you make the
payment to confirm is the payment was
transfer to the address I gave you so
that you can get back to us with
correct information.

I will be waiting to here from you with
the correct info.

Thanks and God bless you,
Mr. David Ray

How Are You?
From: Steve Higgins

Ah hello, thanks for calling, how are
you?
When will my money arrive please?
How are you?

Steve

FOLLOW MY INSTRUCTIONS
From: David Ray

I WANT YOU TO GO TO WERE YOU
MAKE THE PAYMENT AND CONFIRM
FROM THEM WHY OUR ACCOUNT
OFFICER CAN NOT PICK THE MONEY
FROM MONEY GRAM IF YOU CAN
NOT DO THAT WHICH MAINS YOU
DID NOT MAKE THE PAYMENT.

THANK YOU,
MR.DAVID RAY

Sorry
From: Steve Higgins

Hi Ray,

Has you capital locking key become
jammed? I'm really sorry but I find your
emails really difficult to read as you
have used no punctuation and it's all
written in capital letters.

If possible, could you re-write your
previous email using proper
punctuation and grammar so I can fully
understand what you mean.

Thanks,
Steve

I said....!
From: David Ray

Hello,

What I main is this I said the payment
remit on the 26th our account officer
which is Mr. John Nelson could not
pick up the money due to the money
was not send the Abuja Nigeria you
have to go the local money gram were
you make the payment and confirm if
the payment was send to us now and
get back to us.

Thank and have a nice day,
Mr. David Ray,

Sorry
From: Steve Higgins

Hi Ray,

I have just been back to where I made
the payment on the 26th (twenty-sixth),
they said they had no record of my
payment to the Money Gran. The store
I went to is this one... [link to B&Q]

I'm sorry for any delay and confusions
caused by the B&Q staff, please
resolve this as soon as possible (ASAP)
so I can claim my prize winning funds
money.

God bless you and Jesus rest in peace,
I love you,
Steve

No Payment
From: David Ray

With out your money been confirmed
your prize will not be send to you,

Go to any bank that oprate with western union in your country and make this payment today and as soon as you make the payment scan to us the payment slip

I await your response today,

Mr. David Ray

I'll Hunt You Down!
From: Steve Higgins

NO! I've already made the payment at a B&Q Homeware Superstore! So send me my money or I'll hunt you down and lick you in the ass!
Take care,
Steve

Wrong!
From: David Ray

Then you did not make the payment if you can not go there and confirm from them,
Thank you

I'm Sorry
From: Steve Higgins

I'm sorry for getting angry, I am crying at the moment, this is all very upsetting for me (Steve).

I don't have much money and I had to use my savings to pay the £120 and now you are saying you haven't got the money and B&Q are telling me I haven't paid there!

I don't know what to do, I will try to borrow some more money and make another payment, should I try Western Onion instead?

Love,
Steve

Pay Me!
From: David Ray

Yes go ahead and make the payment true western union and get back to us i pray you are not playing with us so you go there and remit the payment and get back to us immediately,

Thank you
From: Steve Higgins

OK, thank you master - thank you for your patience.

I will go to Western Onion immediately.

I also pray back to you in reverse that you are not playing me and my poor starving family.

Steve

Who Are You???
From: Steve Higgins

Dear Sir/Madam/Other,

My name is Steve Higgins, I seem to have several emails from you in my inbox. I have been in hospital for the last two weeks so I am surprised to see that you have been in contacted with me.

It looks like, while I have been away my brother Dominic has been sending emails from my email account.

I am really sorry if he has caused you any problems? I hope he hasn't wasted too much of your time.

Best wishes,
Steve Higgins

P.S. What is this about a lottery win?? I should be so lucky!

PAY ME!
From: David Ray

As soon as you are coming back from work you make the payment true western union and scan to us with the payment information

Payment?
From: Steve Higgins

Hello Sir,

Sorry, what payment is required? As I said, I've been in hospital and it looks like my brother has been using my email account and pretending to be me.

Has he caused some kind of trouble?
What costs has he incurred?

Steve

I'm Upset
From: David Ray

I got your mail and was quite upset
with nature,with the way you wrote it
seems that you are about to loose your
chance of ever becoming a rich
person,this is a fund that could change
your entire family life and your
immediate friends life ^I would like you
to be of good courage^ in line with the
scriptures mind you that the Bible says
and I quote ^it is not of him that runeth
nor willeth but of God that showeth
mercy^ that is what I am talking about
here this is a great chance that God
has created for you, so you should not
ever think about letting it go.

Remeber that the forces of nature
would certainly fight against you when
you are about to make progress in life
so I advice you to look at it very closely
so that your crown would not be talking
away.Remeber that the Bible says and I
quote ^God giveth us power to make
wealth^ this is a life opportunity my
Fellow Brother so act in line with the
right terms and be blessed according
to the riches of our heavenly Father
think about it and get back to me if
possible remain bless.

So you have to be fast about it today.

I will advice you to go and look for
money today so that your cheque can
leave to your door step.

I await for your urgent reply today.

Yours in Service,
Mr.David Ray,

Bad Dominic!
From: Steve Higgins

David, I'm really very sorry if my brother
has been wasting your time.

I have only got out of hospital today,
this is first email I have read from you.

I hope Dominic will not mean that I will
loose this money you speak of.

Yours,
Steve

You're a Winner!
From: David Ray

Hello,

your email address was selected
among the five luck winner all you have
to do to clam this prize of yours you
have to remit the payment for the
delivery of your prize to you door step
the payment has been send to you
your cheek your email you will find the
payment information there,

Thank and have a nice day,
Mr. David Ray,

Hmmm...
From: Steve Higgins

Oh OK thanks David, I'll have a read back through some of these emails later and see if I can work it all out

Thanks for your help,
Steve

You have to PAY ME!
From: David Ray

You have to do that and get back to me immediately,
your prize has been register under the security company that will deliver your prize to your address so get back to us with the payment,

Thank you,
Mr David Rsy,

Are You a Fraudster?
From: Steve Higgins

David,

Obviously I do need the prize money, who wouldn't? But I do need to look in to this further and ensure that this is a valid offer. For all I know you might be some filthy, lying, cheating fraudster (you head about a lot of them on the internet don't you! haha!).

I promise I will look in to this as soon as I get home this evening, if all is fine then it will be no problem transferring the money to you as soon as possible.

Steve

I'm waiting...
From: David Ray

Ok i will be waiting to to get your email immediately today,

Thanks
From: Steve Higgins

David,
Thanks for your ambivalence, I have great news!
As of last night (Saturday), I have become a UK lottery winner! I could be you… it was, LOL! I now have £1.4 million! I am rich beyond my wildest dreams, can you imagine having that kind of money, I bet you'd do anything to get your hands on it.
Well, I'm not a greedy human and don't want to waste anymore of your time so I'd like it if you could instead donate my winnings from your organisation to a worthy charity, perhaps one which deals with the plight of death bats and other airborne rodents.
Steve

For Better Or Worse

I RECEIVED AN EMAIL FROM THE VERY BEAUTIFUL SVETLANA, A YOUNG RUSSIAN LADY WHO WAS LOOKING FOR LOVE AND LUCKILY, SHE'D FOUND MY PROFILE ON A DATING SITE. JOIN ME AS I LEARN ALL ABOUT THIS RUSSIAN TEMPTRESS AND FOLLOW US AS OUR RELATIONSHIP BLOSSOMS.

Salut,
It's Svetlana and I am a 28 years lady. You may be wondering who I am, I found you at site of date and decided find out more about you. I for the first time try to meet man by this method so I decided to try. I am a single lady and I would very much like to learn more about you. I will send a picture in my next letter so you could see what I look like, and I will be happy to get some back of you. I would like to find a serious man for serious relations, someone older than me.

Don't reply to me if you are not single or you got message wrongly.

Hi Svetlana,
I wasn't aware I was on any dating sites but that's fine, it was a pleasurable to receiving your letter and the photograph which came attached to it (the letter). You are VERY pretty and beautiful! I don't often get emails from girls like you where I am.

I am a little older than you, not much, I'm 32. Do you live in London? I only ask as I take it English isn't your first lasagne?

I look forward to talking to you some milk.

Steve
x

Hello Steve,

What is your real name? My real name you already know, my name is Sveta!

Now I tell you about me! I am assured that you wish know it. My native land Russia, and I I live in Russia in my native city in Samara now! Samara is a very beautifull city! I was born I was born in September, 25th, 1987.

Having looked at my photos you will think that there have been many men, but this is not so! I never was married and I do not have children!

I work as the proof-reader in the local newspaper. I correct errors in articles and I give to the editor the ready text. When I went to school, English language was my favourite subject.

I love children and would like to have them in the future.

Write more, do not hesitate, I will be glad to know you!!

I wait for the letter. Sveta!!!

Good hidings,
Again your photo does sexy things to me, you would look sooo hot with a

beard. My real name is Steve or Steve, but you can call me Rich... because I am, hahaha!

That's a coincidental! My birthington day is also September 25th! We are like a match made in Devon! I was born in Quoften which is a small commune about three-eighths outside of London. My nearest Subway is open until 11pm.

I have previously been married, but my marriage came to a very sudden end last year, hence my current situation. That day was also the last time I saw my children, they are resting now.

You are an editor, that sounds like an interesting job, lucky you're not a translator. I find it hard to believe that your favourite lesson was English.

I used to work in banking until, well, you know... Banking this, banking that, general banking really. I'm not sure if I would want any more children, to be honest, I'm not sure if I'd be allowed to after... well, who knows.

I am glad to know you too but you are dog-milk far away? Are you OK with making love through a long distance relationship?

Steve
x

I am glad to tell "HELLO" to my dear friend Steve again! And I hope that it also important for you, as well as for me. I have read your letter with the big pleasure!

Steve I think, that you wanted know more about my interests and a hobby. I will begin one after another. I like to listen to different music. I do not take a great interest in any concrete direction in music.

I very much love cinema, and in particular romantic and historical films. Recently I looked a film "James Camero: Avatar", and it became my favourite film! In this film very good opened theme of love to the nature.

I wish to pass to easier and amusing theme, let's speak about meal!! :-) As I already spoke to you I adore to cook. I take a great interest in a healthy food, I will not write now all dishes which I can prepare because it can occupy all the day! :-) Steve, you like to cook?

Believe to me, you fall in love with Russian kitchen. I would be not against to try kitchen of your country.

I love the nature, and also I love flowers. You like the nature Steve? How you like to spend your free time? Please write to me about it my dear Steve I want, that you knew all about me and also I wish to know all about you Steve!

I wish to ask you about quantity of things, Steve, and I hope, that you will understand my questions and will answer them. I wish to learn more about your interests!

Sveta

Aloe vera Sveta,

It's really nice to hear from you (you), I was worried you weren't going to reply, it has been a few days. Have you been busy? You made me anxiety.

I actually didn't ask about you're interests and hobbies and to be honest, I have very little interest but thanks for sending me that lonnnnng chapter of your autobiography :-)

I like movies too, I very much like romantic historical movies which document the real life relationships between actual people from the past. My favourite is the 1967 romantic classic Bonnie and Clive which tells the story of the turbulent love triangle between television host Clive Anderson, comedian Sandi Toksvig and Bonnie from Big Brother 7.

I don't cook much, I used to but not any more. All the food is served on trays here, we call it "slop", I do miss food.

It's funny you should say about falling in love with a Russian kitchen, that's exactly what happened to my brother. We had a kitchen fitted by the Russian kitchen chain Kukhnya. My brother really fell for it hard, we had to call out the fire brigade after he got his meaty fork stuck in an easy-glide drawer.

Oh, I do love nature so. Sadly nature is something else I am missing. The closest I get to nature now is the yard on recreational breaks but it's not the same as chasing a deer through an open meadow on quad bike.

Please do not mention sport. My father was a tennis player and he left my mother after getting involved with the mens' semi's, it's a touchy subject.

My free time I mostly spend painting, there's also the option to get involved in classes like brush making and working in the license plate factory. So life is pretty varied all things considered.

Hope to hear back from you soon, please don't be so long in to your reply time please, I enjoyment of the talking to you. You are quickly becomming a powerful friend in my life.

Steve

Dear Steve,

I see that we are interested the friend in the friend more and more, and I think that you share my belief Steve. Steve you very good friend, you can understand me, and I think, that it is the important part of a life. Steve, you agree with me, Steve?

Today I have met the old acquaintance, her name Oksana. I have certainly told to it about you Steve. She has certainly become agitated for me, has told that now the Internet is overflowed by a deceit and lie!!! But I have calmed her and have let know, that you very good man, and that you can be trusted!!!!

She asked me to transfer to you hello from her.

My dear Steve, I have understood now, that I very much would like to hear your voice! I think, that it is fine idea. Steve I to wish to tell to you, that the house at me is not present now any phone!!! But I can exploit the phone in the Telegraph! Please tell me your telephone number!!!

I wait your phone number, and very much I believe, that I can soon speak with you. Tell to me please about your friends!!! It would be very interesting to me to esteem about them.

On this good note I finish my letter to you, I hope you it read already today and soon I will see your answer!!!!!

Take care,
Sveta

Tres bien my beautiful Sveta,

It's nice to hear from you with my reading eyes once again, two times a lady.

I do fully agree with you and I mostly understand, although to be honest it is very difficult to understand. Subway have run out of bacon, no BLTs for them today then, hahaha!

But seriously, I would love to hear your voice with my ears, it is not the same seeing your voice in writing. Please call me, it would be magical to talk to in personage. My phone number is this phone number +44 7899 XXXXXX.

Tell Oksana I received her transfer and have reversed it back to her in a gesture of mutual friendship. I prefer salad cream to mayonnaise.

You wish for me to tell you about my friends.... well obviously I haven't seen most of them in years because I'm in here. Some visit from time to time but most of them deserted me after what happened with my ex-wife... well, she's not just an ex-wife, she's an ex-human now - hahaha, I'm sorry I shouldn't joke.

I've made a few friends here though, Norman, Mr. Barrowclough, Lennie, Warren and Governor Venables.

Hope to hear back from you soon or to hear your voice on the telephelone.

Until next time, sleep well and don't have nightmares.

Steve
x

Hi Steve!!

Today I did not sleep all night long and thought only of you. To me was so alone and as I was glad to see again at myself yours e-mail. And I with pleasure speak to you: "HI!!!" Thanks for your letter, I read it some times.

I am so happy to that has met you mine Steve in this big world. I very much value our friendship and is very glad to see you as my friend. I like your understanding through my keys of the keyboard. I never thought and did not know that it is possible to be on friendly terms through letters. Thanks that you have released my soul from chains of a household life.

I write you the full address where I live also the full name.
Rabochii gorodok Street 6
City Samara,
Russian Federation

I hope to obtain from you too your full data?

Thanks you for it my friend Steve!!! I so am afraid to send to you this letter, I do not know your reaction but I wished to tell to you that I feel.

My dear I will call you as soon as possible for me.

Sveta

Trampette du jour to you Sveta!

Crispy Mother of Batman, it's so nice to hear from you again my angular Sveta! Strap yourself in because this email is going to be off the mother loving chain!!

Cola bottles.

I'm sorry to hear you haven't been sleeping, I know that feeling… you should try sharing a cell with three other men! LOL (Laughing On Line).

I'm not sure I would describe you as a friend just yet but I would definitely say that you are some who I have recently come to regard as someone I've emailed a few times. This excites me both mentally in mind and sexually in my pants.

Thank you, I have now obtained your home address successfully, this should come in handy if I'm ever in the Russia area. I'm more than happy to reverse furbish you with my postal addressing.

My address is this address:
Block 5, Cell 497
H.M. Prison Brixton
Jebb Avenue,
London
United Federation of Great Britain
SW2 5XF

I'm looking forward to speaking at you via my telecoms system. Perhaps I could demonstrate some of my imprestinations I can do, for example Lord Jimmy the Savile "now there, now there." LOL (Laughing On Line (again)).

Anyway, I must go my internet allowance is almost up. Please call me before I puke.

In the name of Lord Gregory's Bath I bid thee good partings,

Steve

x

MAYBE IT WAS SOMETHING I SAID, IT SEEMS SVETA DOESN'T WANT TO TALK TO ME ANY MORE. STILL, THERE'S PLENTY MORE CATFISH ACROSS THE SEA.

Love In The Nick Of Time

I WAS CONTACT BY A VERY BEAUTIFUL RUSSIAN LADY BY THE NAME OF AGNESSA, SHE WAS LOOKING FOR LOVE AND SHE FOUND IT. WHAT FOLLOWS IS OUR ROMANTIC EMAIL CORRESPONDENCE.

Hello,
How are you? My name is Agnessa.

Unfamiliar woman sent me a message on the dating site which was your email. I decided to write to you. I'm looking for a man for serious and longterm relations.

If you are interested in me, write to me on my email: vseputem@tarar.biz.ua, I will wait for your letter with impatience, I will tell you more about myself.

Good luck!
Agnessa

Hi,
Thanks for your email, I'm not sure what dating site you found me on, I'm actually on a few sites scattered across the whole galaxy, but it's OK.

I am single, a little older but it sounds like you might not be from my neck of the woodland glens?

Steve
x

Hello!

I am happy to receive your letter and to begin communication with you. I'll be glad if you send me your photo.

I think that you ask yourself why I decided to write you, may be because I'm disappointed by men here. I have heard about people who found their happiness far from the place where they live. I want to find a man for serious relations.

I was born 12 July 1985. I live in the city Pushkino, not far from Moscow.

I work as a nurse in the hospital. I like my work. I'm happy when people recover. I help them to recover, to feel better.

Do you know how it's wonderful to understand that you help people? Sometimes when I have a bad humour, I come to work, help patients and humour becomes better.

I live alone in one-room flat not far from the centre of the town. I like the town where I live very much, it's very nice but i'm sad that i have not met a good man here.

I like to walk around, I prefer active lifestyle. I am very gay and frank.

Well, tell me more about yourself because knowing each other better we can become closer to each other.

You may ask me everything you wish. I finish my letter here and will wait for your reply.

Agnessa

Hello back at you!

Nice to hear from you again, I didn't think I would and thanks for the VERY arousing photo! You look like Maggie Merlin from Barber's Mead! I have reverse attached to you a photo of me, I hope you like it, I did my best birthday smiling!

I'm glad you are looking for a serious relationship, I seem to go through one companion after another, I feel like I've been to the end of the universe looking for my perfect partner.

So, you're a Russonian? That's pretty exotic and slightly erotic, I've never travelled there which is surprising as I have visited many many places, I work as a timelord, so I travel a lot.

It must be very rewarding working as a nurse. I know what you mean about work changing your mood. Sometimes I'm all like "hahaha" and then other times I'm like "ugh" but then when I work it changes me from "ugh" to "hahaha" again. I hardly cry at all now on those days.

I live alone too, I have a pretty spacious place, you wouldn't know it to look at it. From the outside it looks really small, it's surprising really.

I also like to walk a lot please. It's nice to feel that connection to Earth under my feet, it's pretty rare now-a-days with all the flying around all over the place.

You are gay and frank, that's quite a coincidence! I used to be gay too, with a man called Frank but I went a special group at a local church and the cured me.

My age would probably scare you because I don't look as old as I am, I tell people I'm 35 because they'd never believe me if I told them I'm about 900, haha!

Please welcome my goodbye in to your mind as I part with my words on top of you and I aim to read more from you soon with lust.

Steve

Hello!

Thank you for your letter, I'm happy to receive it. How are you? I'm fine.

I know English rather well, I learnt it in the institute. I like languages and would like more of them. I will try to write my letters that you could understand me. As for me, I understand your letters very well.

Well, I want you to tell me more about your working day, it will be wonderful to learn more about you. My working day is usual. I get up at 6.30, take a shower, then make breakfast and gather my things to go at work. I take a

public transportation to get to my work. And I'm at
work at about 7.30. Till 6pm I'm at work. After it I go home, have supper. In the evening I do some works about the house or visit my friends. You can see that I have an ordinary working day.

What is your favourite film? I like 'The City Of Angels,' but my favourite film is 'Brave Heart,' I also like 'Avatar.' Can you tell me about your favourite dish? As for me, I prefer pancakes. I also like salads, ice cream and pizza.

I finish here. I hope to receive your letter soon and I'll answer you with pleasure.

Your Agnessa.

Hello my wonderful balcony!

I'm also fine, how are you? I'm fine. Thanks.

Your English does seem to be good but then, I don't really need to concentrate on language too much, the TARDIS translates everything in my head, it's like a psychic link.

I will happily tell you about my usual working day, it goes like this:
7:00 Wake up
7:10 Poop
7:13 Shower including four minutes for a "personal moment"
7:25 Breakfast (hot coal)
8:00 Travel to different time period or point in the galaxy

From here the time scale sort of goes a bit wibbly-woobly-timey-wimey and it's hard to really say what I did then without getting caught up in some kind of crazy paradox but I usually land back home in this time period at around 6pm and then the rest of my evening...

18:10 "Personal moment"
18:20 Poop 2 (if needed)
19:00 Long burst of crying (usually under water in the bath)
22:30 "Personal moment" (if stamina permits)
23:00 Bed

My favourite movies, that's a tough questions. I like 'Banana Party' the first one was great but I hated 'Banana Party 2: The Splits,' I also liked 'Surprise Funeral' and 'Simply Beef.'

My favourite dish is a brown ceramic one, it has several chips in it but it's still my favourite, I've had it for almost 700 years. It's a replica of one used by the Mighty Jagrafess of the Holy Hadrojassic Maxarodenfoe.

I also finish here, I'm very pleased to have heard from you once more again and please, may I ask a question of you? Do you have any plans to come and visit this country of mine? I assume that is why you are interested in men from this part of the world we call Earth?

Steve
x

Hello, my dear,

How are you? I'm happy to have your new letter.

These days I'm bored a little bit, there are no joyful things around me and your email is like the ray of the sun for me now.

I am looking for a man for long relations but without success. In my country men can't understand women in different ways and it makes me sad that's why i am looking a person through the internet.

I think that letters will help us to learn more about each other and one day we can meet. I hope that we'll make our dreams real.

Please write me as you can. I will wait for your letter with impatience.

Sincerely yours,
Agnessa

Hello Agnessa you rotten gooseberry of my hearts,

You letters also spark extreme arousal in me too, I spend most of my days pressing F26 and holding down the 'L' key on my keyboard to refresh my incoming mail box hoping that I will happen across a refreshed correspondences from your beautiful face.

My body is largely made of water, about 70% in fact.

I'm sorry to hear the men in your part of the galaxy are not of the quality you desire, I have encountered so many different races and species that I feel I am quite well versed in relationships, even inter-species relationships. You'd find it hard to tell I'm not actually human, it's only really my two hearts which gives it away but that just means double of the love for you.

Let's look at the facts. OK, well I've enjoyed speaking to you please.

Steve

Hello my dear Steve.

Thank you very much for your letter, you can't imagine how I'm happy to have it.

I communicate with you not so long but I feel that you are becoming closer to me. I want to communicate with you in any time and more often that's why I want to give you my telephone number, +7901293451 that we can phone me and we can speak with each other and I could hear your voice. Do you like this idea?

I want to know everything about you. What do you like and dislike? I like people that can take care of me and help me in difficult situations. I do not like lie and when someone is lying.

Do you have a lot of friends that you can trust fully? I have a lot of acquaintances but few real friends.

I want to tell you about my family. I have never written you about my family because it's very painful for me. I lived in the town Grozniy, in Chechenskaya Republic., my house was attacked by bandits and they killed my mom and dad when I was 16 years old. After that I could not live there anymore.

I hope that all my failures will finish and I'll find a good man with whom I'll have a real family. I finish here and will wait for your reply.

Sincerely yours,
Agnessa

Alright dog!

Thank you for your phone number, I'm not currently in the same timezone as you, I'm actually in 1930 trying to defeat a rouge Dalek faction who are trying to stop the construction of the Empire State Building in New York. Perhaps I can give you a call later in the week?

What do I like and dislike? Well, I like when small men lick my knees and I dislike pears, soldiers and guns... give me a sonic screwdriver any day hahahahahahahahahaha... ha! (Eggs.)

I don't really have many friend either, I seem to find myself with one companion at a time, I spend a while with her just exploring the whole of space and time but eventually it gets a bit much for them and they go back home.

That's really funny about your parent getting shot, I wish I had been there to see that, it sounds brilliant! I know what it's like though, my parent died in a time war centuries ago, in fact all of my race died in the war. I'm the loan survivor, I watched Gallifrey (my home planet) burn.

Well it's been milky as heck talking to you again and I can't wait to hear from you with my email reading eyes soon. Now go away and get me as much salmon as you can find!

Thanks for being nice,
Steve

Hello my dear,

Thank you for your new letter, it always does my day brighter and I love reading your letters.

I like you very much and i have never heard so many kind words before. I'm so happy and grateful that we found each other through the internet.

I wait our communication by phone with impatience. Well, it seems that my tariff plan doesn't allow me to receive and do calls abroad. Don't worry, I have found the decision of this problem, send me your telephone number and I can call you from my

friend as soon as it's possible. And
finally we could hear our voices.

Tell me what you do at weekends. As
for me, first of all I do the cleaning
around the flat. I like to do it very
much. I also like to go to the cinema.
But sometimes I stay at home in front
of TV.

Tell me how your friends and relatives
would characterise you. Only don't
write yourself. I want your friends or
relatives to answer it. As for me my
friends characterised me like this: kind,
soft (but not always), sometimes a little
silly, but usually enough smart.

I would like to walk with you on the
beach in future. I love the sun, water
and sand. May be? What do you think?

Well, here I am dreaming again. I hope
that our relationship will be more
serious, I hope so.

I must go now and I'll wait for your nice
letter tomorrow.

Kiss you with tenderness,
Your beautiful Agnessa

Hi,

Yes, your kind words make my blood
boil too and receiving your email is like
being hit in the face by a dead owl!

My tariff also isn't an international tariff
which is a shame, it would be good to
hear your voice.

If you'd like to call me from your friend's that would be great, my telephonic number is [my phone number].

At the weekend I mostly cry in to my pillow and try to touch people.

You sound like a bit of an asshole according to your friends if you ask me, haha! My friends and relatives would describe me as mysterious, a time traveller, brave and highly sexual.

I like walking on the beach too and love the sun, in fact I've been there several times. Luckily the TARDIS filters out harmful radiation and the searing heat... although, it's not as hot as you, you evil wench.

What are you doing this weekend? Got lots of milk in ready?

Steve
x

A Witchdoctor Helped Me Become A Real Man

SOMEONE CALLED ERIC MARY FROM THE UNITED STATE OF FLORIDA LEFT A COMMENT ON MY WEBSITE SAYING THAT HIS LOVER HAD LEFT HIM THREE YEARS AGO AND THAT HE APPROACHED A NIGERIAN SPELL CASTER CALLED DOCTOR ABAKA WHO WAS ABLE TO BRING HIM BACK IN TIME FOR CHRISTMAS.

HERE'S WHAT ERIC'S COMMENT SAID...

I am Eric Mary from United State Florida, am so sorry if this is coming late and if you people might have fallen into the wrong hands of scams, because same thing happened to me after my lover left me for three years. I tried everything humanity possible to get him back but it never worked out so I decided to give up the very day I made up my mind to give up I was in a saloon reading a magazine when I saw a testimony from a lady in Texas thanking this great man called Doctor Abaka, how he helped her to bring back her lover I was like for this lady to write this on a magazine meaning this Doctor Abaka is real so I got down is contacted and I called him for help and explained everything to him which then he gave me word of encouragement and I proceeded with him he told me that I will celebrate Christmas and enter the new year with my lover which then I must confess to you all that it really happened I celebrated the Christmas with my love Steven and also enter 2018 with him am just so happy for what this great man has done for me friends clean your tears today and I am proud to tell you that Doctor Abaka will clean your sorrow here his Doctor Abaka contact drabakaspelltemple@gmail.com and you can call him on +2349063230051.

SO, I THOUGHT I WOULD CONTACT THIS MAGICAL DOCTOR AND SEE IF HE COULD HELP ME WITH A PROBLEM I'VE BEEN SUFFERING WITH FOR MY WHOLE LIFE. HERE'S HOW THE CONVERSATION WENT...

Hello Dr Abaka, I saw your comment on a website I visit and wondered if you could help... but it's a bit embarrassing.

Hello, how are you

I'm OK thank you, doctor. My problem is that my two veg are fine, but my meat is somewhat lacking in the portion-size department. I'm short of a full quarter pounder if you know what I mean.

I saw your message and the content was well understood.

I was hoping you might be able to perform some sort of ritual to make it bigger.

I'm assuring you that there is a powerful spell oil which I will prepare for you it has no side effect it will only make your penis bigger as you wise, and once you get the oil all your wises will come through and be able to satisfy a woman which will make every women to run after you the spell oil is not reversible okay! I'm going to prepare it and send it to you in your country and you will receive the oil after sending it okay as soon i get the items needed to prepare the oil spell okay.

Thank you doctor, that sounds excellent!

Send me the following information about you:
Your photo:
Your full name:
Country:
Your address:
Your desires size you wise to have:

I await your response, so that i will tell
you how you will get the oil and the
cost okay!

Thank you, doctor. I've attached the
photo of the "problem," here's
everything else you asked for, I hope
this is OK. My desired size, I don't
know... I don't want to be greedy or big
too big, so anything over three inches
would be fine.
Your full name: Steven Elizabeth
Higgins
Country: United Kingdom of Great
Britain & Wales
Your address: 33 Clapham High St,
London SW4 7TP

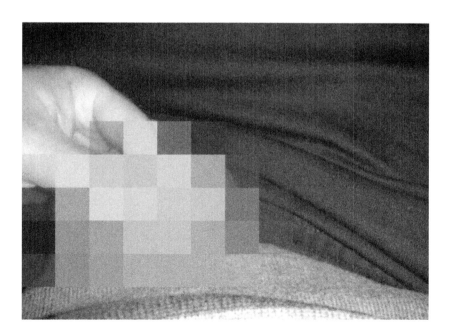

I got your information and you are welcome to my temple once again, and here is a place where you will have solution to your problem, you have make the right choice of contacting me because there is no problem that is been brought to my temple that cant be solved as i believe in my work and my work always speak for me

Cool!

I have done some consultation of the spell and my gods has reveal to me how your problem is going to be solve OK, my gods has require for some specific items that is needed to prepare the spell oil that will help you enlarge your manhood and this items is going to cost you (472) pounds

Wow, expensive voodoo!

Note, that I do not beg or false people to send me money to do their work, rather I will allow them to do according to there heart desire. I have been doing this work for the past 38 years now, and inherited this work from my great grand father, and this work has been past from generation to generation, as I believe in my work so also my work speaks for me because what is behind my spell is very powerful

That is very honest of you, thank you for being so open.

If you are able to send this, i will have to send my temple messenger to go and get me the items from the items sellers from the market then i will carry out your spell preparation OK, and it will be delivered to your address through UPS speed post office once you receive the oil and make use as instructed your heart desire will be granted to you is that OK

Do you think three inches will be big enough?

That depends on your choice. How many inches do you want?

I'm not sure, what size are you?

I think probably 5 or 6

OK, five inches will be good.

If you are ready to continue let me know so that i can send you the information of my temple messenger to send the money to buy the require items needed to prepare the oil spell OK

OK, let's do it! I can't wait to show all my friends!

I have already said you how much it will cost to get the item's I need to use and prepare the oil which will make it 5 inches as you wise. Once you get the herbal oil you will use it to rub your penis everyday after having your bath OK, and you 13 days your manhood will be 5 inches big which is 100% grantee that is going to work

Rub it on my penis? If you can call it a penis! Haha, it's more like a stump!

You will use it to rub, I am showing you the herbal oil which I will prepare for you also

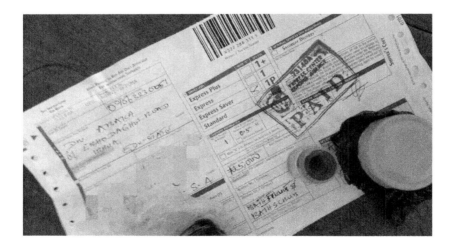

Ummmm surely you shouldn't be revealing the personal details of your clients. I thought you guaranteed privacy and discretion?

Yes am showing you because i help them too

I'm sure you did, but you've also now revealed that Alan Datulier has a small penis. I don't want you sharing my details like this to your other clients. This is very unprofessional and unethical.

You don't have to worry about it what ever I do is between us

Hmmm, I'm not sure Alan Datulier would like you sharing his details.

That's how I work OK

Then, no thank you. I am not interested in your services. I don't want my name and problem shared with others.

They share it because they received a satisfy result from my home. Let me ask you a question my child if you didn't see some one who testify how I help them solved there problem will you have get my contact and seek for help?

Yeah, your website looked professional and you had people's feedback and testimonials on there. I just don't think you should be sharing people's full names, addresses and personal problems without their permission.

I don't share my client personal details
to anyone whose so every I help always
share my good works in there lives

OK, believe you a bit.

My son don't think am not educated ok
I have been helping people with my
spell and herbs for the pass 38 years
and know one has ever come to my
home without a solution to his or her
problems If you want me to help you let
me know okay. I work with trust and
faith to enable a positive result.

Huh? Educated? I didn't say anything
about your level of education or your
abilities. I believe you are capable of
what you say, I just didn't like that you
shared that person's private personal
details and name, that's a breach of
trust.

You have to trust me

I said, I do. If you promise not to share
my details it's OK.

I will not share your details to anyone
all I want is for you to be happy as a
man

Ladies and gentlemen, put your hands
together for Take That!

I promise

> Great, because all I do each night is pray. All I do each night is think, of all the times I've closed the door to keep my love within.

Don't worry your details are safe with me and I assure you that with the herbal spell oil which I will prepare and send to you will enlarge your manhood to 5 inches

> Perfect! Surely we must be in sight of the dream we long to live?

Your heart desire will be granted but before I start with your I need to know if you are ready to make your dreams come through

> If you can't forgive the past, I'll understand that, can't understand why I did this to you. But yeah, happy to continue if that's OK, doctor. Just tell me the song and I'll sing it, you'll be right and understood.

I understand it's ok, I will help you and make your wise come to pass and you will get 5 inches big as you want ok

> That's almost five inches MORE!

If I get this money I can arrange the
item's and prepare the oil to make sure
your manhood is big and it will take 13
days to see the changes

It's a little bit more than I was
expecting it to be actually. I can't really
afford that much at the moment.

My child you need to talk to me how
you can get this oil

Well, help me escape this feeling of
insecurity. I need you so much but I
don't really think you need me. The
thing is, you got to be strong enough to
walk on through the night, there's a
new day on the other side, got to have
hope in your soul.

That's why am here to help people with
there problem because I take your
problems to be mine then put a smile
on your face

Stop being so hard on yourself, it's not
good for your health.

How much do you have now so I can
call the item's seller to keep the
materials for me

Well, all I can really afford at the
moment is about £5, I don't have a job
at the moment, I'm waiting for some

money to come through, but right now I have nothing.

Ok

So the little bit of money I do have, I have to keep to spend on bread, milk, onions, soap, soup, soep. Tonight this could be the greatest night of our lives, Let's make a new start, the future is ours to find.

Try and get money so I can help you.

Just have a little patience, I'm still hurting from a love I lost. I'm feeling your frustration, any minute all the pain will stop. I really wanna start over again, I know you wanna be my salvation, the one that I can always depend.

I needed those materials to prepare the spell oil

I'll try to be strong, believe me I'm trying to move on. It's complicated but understand me.

I understand you

Is there any way you can reduce the price at all?

How much can you get now so I can
know how to help you

> Well, right now only the five British
> pounds, it might take me a few weeks
> to get more. Just hold me close inside
> your arms tonight, don't be too hard on
> my emotions.

Try and get 350 pounds I will complete
the other to get the items when you get
the oil then you can pay the other
balance

> I'll do my best, I'll phone a friend, she
> has laughed it my little dinkle before,
> she might lend me the money out of
> pity.

LATER...

> My friend says she can lend me £300,
> will that be enough?

Ok that will be good if you send 300 I
can be able to get the items from the
seller and begin with the your work
immediately. How long will it take you
to have the money?

> I can get it today. How do I pay? Is
> there a payment form on your website
> or something?

You are to use Western Union or money gram to send the money which I will give you the information to you

Western Union or Money Gram? Aren't those the service that scammers use?!? Don't you have PayPal or a form on your website. Western Union or Money Gram makes you seem very unprofessional.

My child if you need my help I will know

But only scammers use Western Union. EVERYONE knows that!

Western Union is what I use to receive money from people to do there work

Really? Why don't you put a proper payment form on your website TripplePay or Milk Finance.

Use western union or money gram

But that makes you looks like you're a scammer yourself, I'm sure you don't want people thinking that. No one here uses Western Union or Money Gram, it's just for fraud. EVERYONE knows that.

You can pay to bank account it will still be better

OK, that sounds more normal.

You need help to enlarge your manhood with my herbs oil

OK, well if I can get the bank details then, I'll get my friend to send the money straight to you

So if you want to get the oil then we proceed, I will have to call my son. His dose not stay with me here in my home it miles away from my temple.

I don't care.

The easy way I receive money to work is western Union office or money gram so that will be easy and fine by me if you have in your country

But that's what scammers use! No one trusts Western Union here.

Am not fake what I do here is grantee and trusted

Oh heavens to murgatroyd, Batman! The last thing I'd do is call you fake, it's just a bit weird you would use Western Union. You should switch to a trusted payment method like PayPet or KashKollector.

I will know more about that now the
you told me my son. Once I receive
your payment I will prepare the oil and
send to you

Sure thing, just send me those bank deets brother!

Before I start my work there must be
trust and faith in it to enable a positive
result. I am a traditional herbalist My
herbs cure do not recognise long
distance, i have worked on clients from
different parts of the world from
different professionals including
medical doctors, lawyers, academic
professors and among others. Even
those who felt like it wont be possible
received satisfactory results I will take
the time to explain things to you, and
provide you with honest advice, to
what is best for your situation. I do not
pressure anyone to apply my herbs; I
always leave that decision up to you. I
provide you with honest information,
and when or if you decide to move
forward, I am here to help. Thank you
for taking the time to read, I look
forward to your happiness and may the
gods and goddess provide you all your
desires.

Regards
Dr Abaka

What's that?

When you need the herbal oil to
enlarge your manhood let me know I
have works to do

                Well yeah, I know that. We've been
                talking about that for hours. Please
                could I get the bank details to send the
                money? My friend, Lulu says she'll
                send ASAP possible.

My son bank account details
Account name: Kelvin Ojo
Account number: 6239954508
Swift code is: FIDTNGLA
Bank name: Fidelity Bank PLC

                Perfect, thank you. I should be able to
                make that payment online on the
                internet systems.

OK when you are done let me know

                Thank you, doctor - thoctor. We need
                to be quick, my penis is almost
                inverted today!

Once you are done sending let me
know immediately

                Yes, ma'am.

OK

OK, that has been sent to your financial world

You mean?

No, I'm friendly. You have the cash prizes monies?

What do you mean?

The monies I sent you.

Have you sent the money already?

Yes, here is a screen grab from the bank….

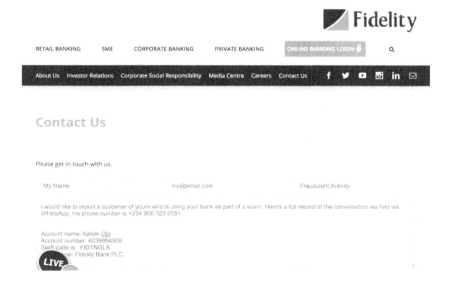

Haaaaa do you think am stupid fool

Well.... yeah, actually.

Idiot you will run mad as long as I live

OK, bye. Nice chatting with you x

A FEW DAYS LATER DR. ABAKA EMAILED ME WITH A SOME SCREEN SHOTS OF A WEBSITE HE'S MADE TO EXPOSE AND SHAME ME, IT FEATURES MY NAME AND A FAKE ADDRESS. I DON'T THINK HE'S ACTUALLY PUT IT LIVE.

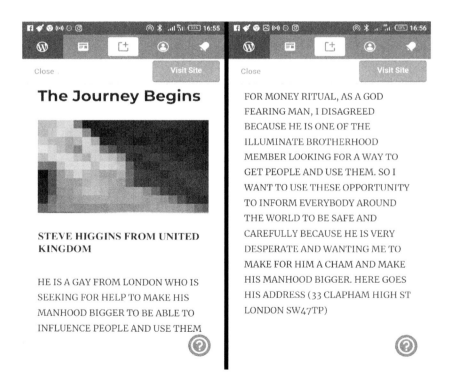

The Journey Begins

STEVE HIGGINS FROM UNITED KINGDOM

HE IS A GAY FROM LONDON WHO IS SEEKING FOR HELP TO MAKE HIS MANHOOD BIGGER TO BE ABLE TO INFLUENCE PEOPLE AND USE THEM

FOR MONEY RITUAL, AS A GOD FEARING MAN, I DISAGREED BECAUSE HE IS ONE OF THE ILLUMINATE BROTHERHOOD MEMBER LOOKING FOR A WAY TO GET PEOPLE AND USE THEM. SO I WANT TO USE THESE OPPORTUNITY TO INFORM EVERYBODY AROUND THE WORLD TO BE SAFE AND CAREFULLY BECAUSE HE IS VERY DESPERATE AND WANTING ME TO MAKE FOR HIM A CHAM AND MAKE HIS MANHOOD BIGGER. HERE GOES HIS ADDRESS (33 CLAPHAM HIGH ST LONDON SW47TP)

Becoming All-Powerful With An Unforgettable Illuminati Finger Ringer

DO YOU FANCY GETTING A FINGER RING FROM AN ACTUAL MEMBER OF THE ILLUMINATI? WELL TODAY IS YOUR LUCKILY DAY, I WAS RECENTLY CONTACTED BY AN AGENT WHO COULD GIVE ME ONE, AND I'M GOING TO SHARE HOW IT WENT WITH YOU.

THIS ALL STARTED WHEN A MYSTERIOUS MAN CALLED JACK JEFFERSON LEFT A COMMENT ON A FACEBOOK POSTS I WROTE ABOUT THE ILLUMINATI. THE BADLY WRITTEN COMMENT SAID:

Hello, I am Jack Jefferson by name, am a member of the great Illuminati brotherhood, Do you want to join the Illuminati and become rich and influential in life…Money is not an issue with us, join us today and kick out your financial problems with a monthly salary of $500,000. Your Finacial welfare is our aim. With us you financially free and stable contact the grandmaster on whatsApp :the head office with +17542127686. Immediately Mr Jack

SO, I SENT "MR JACK" A MESSAGE ON WHATSAPP. BELOW IS OUR FULL CONVERSATION WHICH WAS SPREAD OUT OVER ALMOST 48 HOURS, WASTING PLENTY OF HIS TIME.

> Hello, Mr Jack. I saw your comment on my post about the Illuminate LTD and hoped you might be able to help me to join please.

Okay am going to help you out only if you are interested to do the necessary things

> Well, I think I would like that, obviously it depends what the necessary things are.

NOTE: THERE ARE NO BLOOD OR
HUMAN SACRIFICES IN THE
ILLUMINATI. YOU CAN BE ANY
RELIGION YOU WISH FOR,
CHRISTIAN. MUSLIM, OTHERS.

Welcome to The illuminati World ▲
Bringing the poor, the needy and the
talented to limelight of fame and riches.
Get money, fame, powers, security, get
recognized in your business, political
race, rise to the top in whatever you
do, be protected spiritually and
physically!

All these you will achieve in a twinkle of
an eye when you get initiated

> Oh, I thought the Illuminati were
> famous for human sacrifice. What
> about all the celebrities you kill? Like
> Michael Jackson, Prince, Frank
> Sidebottom, Neil Buchanan, Cilla
> Black, The Krankies, John Lennon,
> JFK, KFC etc?

We don't kill anyone here ok

> What? Everyone knows you do! It's OK, I don't mind.

Are you not interested anymore?

> Yeah, I'm saying it's OK if you kill
> celebrities. I don't mind that. I'm a big
> fan of your murdering ways.

We don't use human sacrifice here OK
you need to trust me

> I don't understand. Are you sure you're
> from the Illuminati? EVERYONE know
> the Illuminati get their control and
> power by murdering those that stand in
> their way.

I am not like that ok

> Oh well, don't worry then. I was
> obviously lied to before. I thought that's
> what the Illuminati was all about. My
> main reason for joining was to help
> sacrifice celebrities.

OK

> Sorry, someone must have lied. Good luck, bye.

Are you not interested anymore brother
you need to trust me OK nothing we
happen to you

> I want to join to help sacrifice
> celebrities but you say you don't do
> that.

You can choose to be rich not famous ok

> I don't care about fame and money. I
> want power. I already have money and

riches after my uncle's accident... it was Noel Edmond's fault and I want revenge.

Am going to help you out so that you can help the sacrifice celebrities ok

Really? Why did you lie before? You said you didn't do that?!? I'm confused.

I think you was playing with me that's why

Oh heck, no! I would never play with a member of the Illuminati.

You said you want to stop is right don't worry I'm going to give you the power to stop it and you need to be serious about this ok don't take everything as joke

I'm not joking... you're confusing me! If you kill celebrities, I will join. If you don't kill celebrities, I'm not interested in joining. Clear?

Why do you want the celebrities dead?

I said, because of my uncle's accident. I want revenge. My uncle was killed by a huge falling fibreglass volcano on a mock tiki island set as part of a television prank. We got compensation, a lot of compensation, but that's not good enough. Edmonds needs to pay!

I'm going to help you to revenge your uncle dead on one condition don't let anyone know about this ok

OK, thank you very much! I am willing to do whatever it takes, even sexual favours.

Alright, that's good

Thanks!

Alright. You need to fill a form right away ok

Yes, ma'am

OK good

 THE ILLUMINATI ONLINE

REGISTRATION FORM. 🔺
*NAME..........
*AGE..........
*GENDER..........
*STATE..........
*COUNTRY..........
*STATE.........
*2PHOTO........
*OCCUPATION..........
*MONTHLY INCOME..........
*MOBILE NUMBER..........

We want you to send the info here

 so we can start your membership registration

Will I need to send you a photo of my penis like when I joined the Freemason? I don't mind but I don't want it being plastered around Dundee again.

No you don't You need to fill the form right away ok

OK, great. I am doing that right now

Alright. Just fill the form and send it to me ok

Yes, I am doing that right now

Alright

Here you go ma'am...
*NAME: Steven Elizabeth Higgins
*AGE: 32
*GENDER: Male
*STATE: Happy
*COUNTRY: United Kingdom of Great Britain & Wales
*STATE: Still happy
*2PHOTO: Will send separately
*OCCUPATION: None
*MONTHLY INCOME: None
*MOBILE NUMBER: You have it

OK good

Thank you, I'm glad you like it, my love. Oh, I'm so sorry! I didn't send the photos you asked for! Shall I send them now?

Alright you are going to be given a magic ring

A fingering?

With the magic ring you can revenge your uncles dead

Yes, a finger ring?

Yes. For you to get the ring you need to pay for a fee

OK, like a donation to the brotherhood?

Because without you paying for that you can't get your magic rings

That's fine. I wouldn't expect anything for free.

The magic ring we are giving you represent power and to kill. You are going to pay for the magic ring before we can send it to you ok

Yes, you said.

i don't get you

You already said I have to pay for it, several times. I was saying I understand.

Am going to help you out with some money for the ring you are going to pay the remaining yourself

It's OK, you don't have to help out, really. I don't expect anything for free. How much will it cost please?

It will cost you 100 pounds. Can you afford the money?

Yeah, that is cheap! Look, this one on eBay is much more expensive.

Ok. You are going to pay the money through money gram transfer

OK, Money Gram. That's fine. So, to be clear, that's £100 GBP?

yes

Noel Edmonds has no idea what's coming to him! OK, do I need an account number or something?

you are expected to go to bank or store tell them that you want to make payment through moneygram

Yeah, I understand

Am going to send you the money gram transfer details that you are going to use to make the payment ok

OK. Will it hurt?

No

Is it possible for me to get two of the rings please? One for my brother too? He really hates Anne Robinson.

OK you are going to pay for the two which is 200 pounds. ok

OK, perfection

What do you mean by that?

You don't understand that?!? Where are you from?

I understand it ok

I should think so! Only a dumb bum
wouldn't understand that, LOL!

Am going to send you the money gram
transfer details right now ok

Hit me with it

MONEY GRAM TRANSFER DETAILS
Receiver Name: OHIWELE AKHERE
Receiver Country: NIGERIA
State: EDO STATE
Amount: 100 pounds
Text question: for
Text answer: benefit

After making the payment

Send me these details below
Sender's name:
Sender's country:

Capture the slip and send me the
photos. Send me the number MTCN
and it's the reference number

Where it says "send me these details
below" all the details are empty.

After making the payment you are the
one that is going to send me the your
name and your country that is what it
means

You already know my name and country

You are going to send me the name
you use to make the payment ok

That will be my name and you already
have that and my country.

OK. So when are you making the payment?

Well I obviously can't do it tonight, no
where will be open

OK. So when will you do it

Is there a chance someone like Dermot
Murnaghan or Paul O'Grady might find
out what I'm planning and try to stop
me?

No they can't ok

OK thanks. I know Paul O'Grady in
particular can be quite a problem

What is the time there

It is 6:27pm o'clock according to my
Casio DX Sports watch that Trevor
McDonald gave me.

OK so you are going to make the
payment by tomorrow right?

Not by tomorrow. I'll make the payment tomorrow.

OK good. By what time?

I'll do it first thing when the banks open
at 9am o'clock

Alright

Is it OK if I tell Clive Anderson? He's
going to be helping me.

Alright

Thanks, I'll give him a call. I'm sure he'll
be very helpful.

Once you make the payment tomorrow
just let me no ok

You mean "know?"

So that we can confirm your payment

Yeah, it's "let me know" not "let me no"

Yes

I thought Illuminati was supposed to mean 'the enlightened' - you don't seem very enlightened but my speilling, and, gramer is excelloid so I'll will be a worthy addition to the brotherhoode.

that is good

I'm going to chat with you tomorrow by 9am o'clock OK make sure you make the payment ok

Not by 9am, AT 9am. The bank doesn't open until 9am.

Alright

Enlightened? LOL!

Good night brother

THE NEXT MORNING AT EXACTLY TWO MINUTES PAST NINE O'CLOCK, MR JACK GOT BACK IN TOUCH...

How was your night brother?

Good thank you my lord, I had Pam St. Clement and Clive Woodward over for a cheese and wine night. How about you?

I hope you have not forgot that you are making the payment today?

Of course not, I want that ring

OK. The time is 9am

Sure is, the bank opens now. So I'll get ready and stroll down.

So are you going now?

In a bit, yeah. I'm not quite ready yet.

I hope you brother is fan?

Fan?

Ok

What do you mean? You hope my brother is fan?

What is the matter brother

I don't understand what you said, "I hope you brother is fan?" - what does this mean?

I said if your brother is ok

No you didn't. You said fan??? FAN?

OK it was a mistake

So you meant to type "OK" but it came
out as "FAN" hahaha, idiot!

What about your mom

She is FAN, AHAHAHAHAH!

is this a joke?

Yeah.

Just go and make the payment so that
your ring will be sent to you ok

Oooooh, someone's grumpy this
morning! I'm just eating my breakfast.

Once you make the payment just let me no ok

No? Let you no?

Know

Ahhhh, OK. Yeah, sure will.

Alright

I'll head down to the bank soon, I'm sure everything will be FAN.

Alright

That was a joke again... I don't think you got it. You don't have much of a sense of humour do you Mr Jack?

Once you are done let me know ok

You said that already

okay

I THEN WENT BACK TO SLEEP FOR ANOTHER HALF AN HOUR.

Have you make the payment?

No, i fell back to sleep, I had a late night. Pam kept me up all night doing her cheese impression. You should see her brie, hilarious! There's no rush though, I'll sort the payment in a bit.

Your ring is ready right away ok

Why the rush?

Nothing

Can you send me a photo of the rings please? I'll get up and go now. Sorry, I wasn't expecting such a late night last night.

OK

Where's the other?

That is the magic ring this is your own ok

But I'd like to see a photo you took of them together so I know they are ready like you said. That photo of is just off of the internet.

The other are in Nigeria

OK, get whoever has them to take a photo, I will pay extra for your time.

You are the only person who will have given this ring

Cool, sounds magical. I'd still like a photo of the two you have ready for me together before I send the money, thanks.

Are you making the payment or not?

Yeah, of course. I'd just like to see the rings first.

Alright

Thanks

Am waiting ok

OK

Brother we are not joking here ok you need to take everything serious

I am serious, that's why I am obtaining all the details I need to make a serious and informed purchase. Ask Jeremy

Paxman, he'll tell you, I'm alway serious.

As soon as you make the payment this thing is going to work out and you're the one that's going to enjoy it

I'm not paying until I see what I am buying. You might not even have the rings.

I have it brother if you are not interested let me know you said that you are going to make the payment yesterday right

Not IT.... THEM! I want two. This is why I need proof you have two for me. I just wanted to see the rings I'm buying, I still want to buy them from you, if you can't do that then I'm not sending the money.

If you are not interested you can go OK

I am VERY interested. If you can still help me that would be great.

If you don't want to make the payment then forget about everything ok

I DO WANT TO MAKE THE PAYMENT!

Go and look for another person ok

> I have the money ready, I even offered to pay you MORE if you can sort this out today. Would it help if I got Bill Oddie to phone you? He can vouch for me.

Do you think you are playing here?

> I don't know, you are wasting my time a bit. I have told you I want to buy, I was going to pay you this morning. Unless you are ready to help me out then I am not interested. If you can sell me the rings, then great, I will send you the money.

Go and make the payment first ok

> Look, I'm good friends with Nick Ross from 'Watchdog' and he says I shouldn't pay you anything until you send me a photo of the rings, and he should know!

After making the payment am going to send you the ring

> It's a simple request. I am buying something, I want to see it before I buy it. Why can't you send a photo? Either you want my money or you don't.

I don't need your money OK

OK, I'm sorry we couldn't work this out. Best of luck in future. Bye.

What am i using your money for

Sorry? I don't know how my money will be used, I assume it will go back into the brotherhood. Perhaps help with the upkeep of temples, or buy more books for the sacred library.

Boy are you playing with the brotherhood

What are you talking about?!? I'm trying to buy two rings. Why won't you sell them to me???

mind the way you speak boy

Don't call me boy, idiot. I'm a wealthy and respected business man, you will talk to me as such. Now, are you going to sell me these rings?

SUDDENLY, MR JACK WENT QUIET.

Answer me, cow!

Have you make the payment of one

I told you, I will make the payment when you send me a photo of them so I know they are in your possession. Would you buy something without seeing it first?

The great brotherhood Illuminati kingdom is not fool boy

Well you are a fool. I'm offering you money and you won't take it. Idiot. Stop messing around with me, this is not a joke!

your money don't have any value in my body boy

How much do I need to pay you to get these rings?

I if you want to get the rings go and make the payment so that all this will stop without that then look for another person

I want to see a photo of them first. If you can't do that, then I'm sorry, I can't buy from you.

I wanted to take you as my son but you disappoint me

So, I can call you mum? Well I'm very sorry that I have disappointed you. I only wanted to see a photo of the rings, if we can't move past that then we will have to part ways. Best of luck in the future. Have a good day, sir.

MR JACK THEN REALISED THAT THIS WASN'T GOING TO GO ANY FURTHER IF HE DIDN'T SEND ME THE PHOTOS OF THE TWO RINGS HE'D PROMISED ME.

That is the rings

HAHAHA! I'm sorry, it seems you are unable to help. Good bye my love.

Good bye

Thanks for your time. Once again, I'm sorry we couldn't work things out. Take care.

Alright bye

Bye

Alright

Thanks

Ok

Good luck with all your future projects.

Alright

Why do you keep saying that? Can I
help you with something?

Why are you still chatting

Every time I say bye you say "alright."

Stop chatting with me

OK, ma'am. Thank for your help and
good luck in future. Bye.

An African Love Doctor Cured My Broken Relationship

A MAN NAMED DR. HASSAN LEFT A COMMENT ON MY WEBSITE SAYING HE COULD HELP ME FIND LOVE WITH A MAGIC SPELL AND LOVE RITUAL, SO I THOUGHT I'D PUT HIM TO THE TEST. HIS COMMENT READ...

Are you disappointed in life you have tried everything but no solution for what is trebling your life? Here is the best Dr. Hassan to help you +1(209) 213 3040

Dr. Hassan has got a good reputation from all over Africa and for so many years and now is here to help you and here are some of his work: Lost love spells, love spells, money spells, lost property, get child spell, attraction spells, divorce spells, revenge spells, win lotto spells, ring of powers and control magic.

Call or text +1(209) 213 3040 or duprixcamel@gmail.com

SOUNDS LIKE HE HAS SOME PRETTY IMPRESSIVE POWERS, SO I SENT AN INTRODUCTION TO THE EMAIL ADDRESS HE'S GIVEN TO SEE IF HE COULD ME IMPROVE MY LIFE.

> Hello, is this Dr. Hassan? I saw your comment on YouTube and wanted to know if your spells and potions are real because I badly need one. Can you help?

Yes I am doctor Hassan and how may I help you?

> Sorry, I've been away for the weekend with my twin step sister, so didn't see your reply. I am interested in obtaining a love potion if possible... and details on how it works.

Send me your full names, date of birth and photo and same for the one you

need to use the spell on, then I will
consult my oracle.

Thank you, doctor. I am.... Steven
Elizabeth Higgins - 22 May 1984. She
is Emily Peter Andre - 19 December
1987. I've attached the photos.

I already consulted my oracle and I will
need to do a binding love spell for you,
you will see the results three days after
I cast the spell. I will need a few items
to do the portion it will cost about
$115.

Heck, the oracle sure is quick! OK, can
you tell me what items you need and
how it will work? I am very keen to
marry Emily ASAP.

I need an African talisman and three
cowries, I will do a command on the
talisman and I will send it to you, once
you say your desire on it, you will start
to see how she will start showing much
love and concern for you, but you can
also contact me anytime you wish to
deactivate the spell.

Oh, I thought you were an expert in
this. I assume because you don't have
these things that you're never
performed this spell before? Is there
any guarantee it will work?

What? This is something I have been doing for years, this is because the items are hard to come by, but here you are sure of full results. Once the spell is casted, I will mail the talisman to you through UPS and you will make wishes to it and you will see how powerful it works.

Oh, so you send the items to me after? I understand now. I just didn't understand why you wouldn't have had these items from the last time you performed that spell.

What is the best way to pay? Do you have a website or something Also, do you have any testimonials from people you've help previously, as it's quite a bit of money it would just be good to hear how you have helped others.

Get to me through WhatsApp on +237676483295, I will call you and let you know all you need to know.

I am scared to talk to you, you are a witch doctor, You might use your satanic powers and hypnate me.

No I only have to help people, I cant harm you, instead I am working to help you out have your heart desire. I am going to help you, I am not evil as you might think.

OK, I believe you. My friend Tony Crisp gave me an idea! Why don't you do a spell to bring me wealth! I'll give you half of the money that I get and you can use that money to perform my love spell!!

Yes it's possible, and it's a good idea, but you will need also need to pay for the items needed to get the money spell done.

OK, no problem. How to I go about doing this please?

You can go to any African store in your city once you buy the African talisman and three cowries, then you can send the to me I will use it to perform the love spell.

OK, I can do that. Where should I send them?

When you get them I will give you my shrine address in Cameroon. Let me know if you can get the items this weekend.

Yes, professor doctor, sir.

THE SCAM IS OBVIOUSLY THAT HE WANTS ME TO BUY THESE ITEMS FROM HIM, SO I THOUGHT IT WOULD BE FUNNY TO CLAIM I COULD GET THE ITEMS WITHOUT HIS HELP. THEN WHAT WOULD THE SCAM BE? TWO DAYS LATER...

Hello, did you get the items?

Yes, I have them now. Are these OK?

The cowries are okay but the talisman
should be of ancient African origin so o
can give you my shrine address so you
can send to.

It was from an antique store, it cost
$250 so I assumed it must have been
quite old. Can you let me know what
type of thing I should be getting, I can
sell this one on eBay.

That's really expensive, I can get the
items here for about $160, you need to
sell that one.

I don't think the man in the shop would
have been trying to con me, that's the

kind of thing that happens on the internet! LOL (laughing online)

Okay, I just wanted to be sure we are using the right materials for the spell, rather than use something that will not work, so send it to me using DHL.

OK...

Send using this address,
Country: Cameroon
City: yaounde
Zip code: 00237
Telephone: +237676483295

No house number or street? How will it get to you??

Yes, when it gets here, they will call me on phone and I will go get it from their office.

OK, I'll try tomorrow but I'm not too sure if FedEx or similar will even let me send it without a full address. I'll let you know.

THE NEXT DAY...

Hello, have you gone there to send the items?

No, they said the address wasn't a valid addressment system.

Send them to via FEDEX, Cameroon, bamenda, 00237, big babanki.

OK, great success!

Did you send the items? I need the tracking number.

No, it's 2:30am the meat shop is closed.

OK, send them in the morning , make sure you stay online.

It's Sunday tomorrow, nowhere will be open apart from church and Bargain Booze.

Okay, then tomorrow Monday make sure you send them, I look at the photo of the items you send. Is that a wooden talisman and how old is that piece?

It was from an antique store, it cost $250. The man (called Alverk) said it was from the cretaceous period.

I am not sure of that, I guess you will have to go refund it, I will have to get the items my self so I be sure of what I am getting.

No, it's OK. They had loads to choose from, some were REALLY old. I think they are cheaper here so I don't mind getting it.

I am saying so because I know the items when I get them my self, if you insist on getting it then no problem but if I perform the rituals and it doesn't then just know the items were not authentic.

Oh codding heck! Can you send me the links to them and I'll buy them?

I said I will go get them from the market thing I can do is give you the email of one of the suppliers I already contacted.

But, sir, I was just trying to be helpful. We have many occult stores here that sell antique items very cheap. English is my first language, I assume it is not your dumb dumb plop head.

What??? You call me dump? I told you the items here cost $200.

No, I didn't use the word dump at all.

And this has taken long, I should have been done with this before if you would just let me get it from the local suppliers.

Well, I'd like to know what you are buying and how much it is going to be?

I am buying an ancient African talisman, three cowries, and love portion.

Yumm! One portion of love please! How much will each of those items cost, your witchyness?

The talisman should be $115, cowries $15 and the love powder $70.

OK, great success! So this time next month I could have three beautiful human baby children of my own with my lovely wife what did a love on me!

Yes, when you see the results then you can do a donation to my organisation.

Sounds excellent. I will be sure to make a sizeable donation to your witch doctoring cause.

So when are you making the payment for the items, so I can perform the rituals maybe today or tomorrow?

I could have done today but since you've put the option out there, I'll go for tomorrow if that's OK. How do I pay you?

It's better you go today so I can secure the items now, you make the payment through Western Union.

That's not very secure though is it? I thought only fraudsters and scammers use Western Union? Can't we use PayPal or Rowtox?

Yes, its true its not secure as you said, but I don't have any other means to receive funds from where I am, there is no PayPal or whatever.

Oh, no thanks then. I'd rather use a trusted payment method. You should really get yourself set up on one, it makes you look like a scammer.

I have partner in town that receives PayPal but he demands extra charges, but for him to pay me $200 for the items then you will need to send $215.

That's OK, I'd rather send it via a secure method. PayPal offers buyer's protection so I can get a refund if you vanish without delivering anything, LOL.

I will give you his PayPal but not once you see the results then you will send my donation via Western Union.

OK. So, what should I do now? I am eager to get this process moving?

The person said he no more uses PayPal but I have also contacted a supplier still here in the US but he's giving the items for $250 and you will pay him through Money Gram in the US and he will receive the funds and send the items to me, then I do you spell simple.

No no no. Money Gram is another one that scammers used. If he is in the US, I could just do a Wobax or Lampfer straight to his bank account, or visit his store.

I can guarantee you that I am a genuine spell caster and I work only with trusted partners, you seems to have so much fear, but I don't blame the is just that you are making the process more complicated.

I'm very sorry to hear that I am complicating things, that is the last thing I want to do. The problem is, you see a few months ago I tried to join the Illuminati with a man I was speaking to on WhatsApp. Just like you he left a comment on my website. I had to send him $1200 to buy items for my initiation ceremony. I paid and then he didn't speak to me again, I don't know if he fell ill or died or something, but the bank said they couldn't get my money

back and said I should use secure
payment in future like PayPal or Grindr.
So, I am sorry, but that is my only
options.

Oh sorry to learn about that, list I can
never do such a thing and I am here
just to help you, nothing else, only for
you to get the results and you want and
send my donation.

Bless your ass, doctor. So, are we able
to proceed in some way? Once your
magic has worked and I know you are
real, I am more than happy to make a
VERY generous donation to your
foundation. Money is no object to me, I
have everything I want in life.
Expensive cars, multiple houses, all
that is missing is the love of my dearest
Emily lady.

You must pay me Money Gram or
Western Union, it is the only option if
you want my help.

I cannot send money in an insecure
way again. This is why Emily left me in
the first place. She was angry that I
gave money away without checking
with her and she left me, I just want her
back.

I just want you to have my trust, I will
prove to you who I am and how
effective my spells works, all I need is
just to get the items and I will do the

spell and within three days you will see results , I will give you my private number so we can keep in contact.

> OK, I believe you, but is there anyway you can demonstrate your magical powers to me?

Yes, I need your full names and date of birth and just the same info for Emily, then you will see my powers.

> Thank you doctor, thoctor. I've already sent you that information. I will send a donation or the money once I know you are real.

Yes, as I told you , I just need the items, are you still able to do the payment for the items today?

> No, I can't pay the ways you've suggested unless I know you are real. That's why I asked if you could show me you really have powers? Can you make something move in my house or give me a sign using magic?

Get me through WhatsApp +237676483295 just text me now.

I THOUGHT IT WOULD BE FUN TO START ANOTHER CONVERSATION WITH THE SCAMMER ON WHATSAPP, BUT I'D PRETEND TO BE SOMEONE COMPLETELY DIFFERENT.

> Hello is this Doctor Hassan?

Yes this is the photo of my son on his graduation

Oh

Anyway let's move on

Yes please

So what I was saying is that I want the items as of now

Items?

But I tried to let you know my oracle is an ancient oracle I inherited from my grand fathers.

What do you mean?

So it's no joking place for me, I go there strictly with permission from the gods to grand peoples request. That's why we don't charge any fee for our services.

Sorry, I don't know what you mean. I just saw your message on a forum I read. I wanted to find out about your "get child spell."

If I take money from you, then the spell will not work, so what I am saying is

that you should just let me have the
items, its simple.

I don't know what you mean. Which
items? Are you Doctor Hassan?

I am Doctor Hassan you have been
communication with on email.

No, I haven't emailed you yet.

Yes I have told you I can help you with that.

I saw your comment on a forum, you
said you can do a spell to get a baby
but sorry, I must have the wrong
person.

Oh no, its just I have a mix up. I cast all
types of spells.

**AT THIS POINT I REPLIED TO HIS EMAIL SAYING, "I DON'T HAVE WHATSAPP, SORRY DOCTOR"
AND THE CONVERSATION CONTINUED ON WHATSAPP WITH ME POSING AS A DIFFERENT
POTENTIAL VICTIM...**

Oh good.

Including the one you need

We would really like a baby, we saw a
really nice one called Graham. He
belongs to a lady from the Murder
Club. Can you get me that baby?

Oh yes is that the one you need?

Yes, he is a powerful child. We want to sacrifice him. Offer him up to Satan, I'm sure you understand as a witch doctor.

Yes, I know but it will cost you expensive.

It's OK. I have just the payment for you. How would you like to live forever alongside the dark lord in Hell? I can guarantee you a place at his side. How does that sound?

You need to pay the right amount.

You will be the most powerful African man ever. The dark lord will share his powers with you and make your penis three feet long. Also you get unlimited free tea and coffee. What do you say? Are you in?

But who are you?

Just call me The Master, my true identity will be revealed in the next life.

You are in the wrong place. Sorry I am not interested.

I know but soon I will transition into Hell and I vow to take you with me if you are ready. You don't not want unlimited power?

Yea, because you don't know me

I know you have the powers I need, you are a dark wizard like me? You know I cannot do spells to benefit myself but if you help me, I can help you. Just think... a one hundred dollars worth of gold!

I understand but I cant help you and you can't help me

Oh, your powers are not real like mine? You know I have the power to hex if you refuse? I was hoping it wouldn't come to this.

You made a mistake

You have made a mistake in not helping me. I will begin my incantations at midnight and lay my hex on you. This is your last chance to help me...

You are so funny

BLOCKED.

Black Balled By The Nigerian Branch Of The Illuminati

THIS ISN'T THE FIRST TIME I'VE BEEN INVITED TO JOIN THE ILLUMINATI AND IT'S NOT THE FIRST TIME I'VE REPLIED TO AN OFFER AND HAD A DISCUSSION WITH A REAL MEMBER OF THE ACTUAL ILLUMINATI.

AS ALWAYS, THE INITIAL INVITE WAS POSTED IN A COMMENT ON MY WEBSITE... AS YOU'D EXPECT. THE SPAMMY MESSAGE GAVE A NUMBER TO CONTACT VIA WHATSAPP, SO I THOUGHT I'D GET IN TOUCH AND SEE WHAT THEY HAD TO OFFER AND SEE IF I HAVE WHAT IT TAKES TO JOIN THEIR RANKS.

THE COMMENT WAS POSTED BY A FACEBOOK USER NAMED JAMES TRACY, AND IT READ AS FOLLOWS:

GREETINGS FROM THE GREAT GRAND MASTER! IN REGARDS OF YOU BECOMING A MEMBER OF THE GREAT ILLUMINATI, WE WELCOME YOU. FREEMASONRY GREAT ILLUMINATI TEMPLE OF MONEY AND POWER, JOIN THE ILLUMINATI

Are you a business man or woman, political, musician, student, the you want to be rich, famous, powerful in life, join the Illuminate brotherhood cult today and get instant rich sum of. 1million dollars in a week, and a free home. any where you choose to live in this world and also get 10,000,000 U.S dollars monthly as a salary BENEFITS GIVEN TO NEW MEMBERS WHO JOIN ILLUMINATI.

1. A Cash Reward of USD $500,000 USD
2. A New Sleek Dream CAR valued at USD $300,000 USD
3. A Dream House bought in the country of your own choice
4. One Month holiday (fully paid) to your dream tourist destination.
5. One year Golf Membership package
6. A V.I.P treatment in all Airports in the World
7. A total Lifestyle change
8. Access to Bohemian Grove
9. Monthly payment of $1,000,000 usd into your bank account every month as a member
10. One Month booked Appointment with Top 5 world Leaders and Top 5 Celebrities in the World
If you are interested email: barryilluminati66@gmail.com us now OR call mr Barry now on this number +(234)08141804288 OR WhatsApp him on +(234)08141804288.

TIME FOR ONE MORE TRY? I HAD TO GET IN TOUCH.

Hello, is this Mr Barry?

Yes, how are you doing?

Ah hello, I am good thanks. And firstly, may I ask how are you?

I am fine. How many I help you piz

Great. And first of all may I say, Mr Barry, what is your first name? And how are you today?

How many I help you piz

I saw your message about joining the Illuminate club and wondered if it was a real offer.

Ok, are you really interested to join the illuminati?

Yes, if it's a real offer, then yes.

OK, send me this details now
Full name:
Sex:
Age:
Country:
State:
Your picture:
Occupation:
Monthly income:

Your purpose of joining the illuminati:

OK, but please can you tell me your first name so I know who I am talking to please?

My name is Mr Barry

Oh, that's a bit vague. Why can't you tell me your full name? I'm not really happy handing over all my details if you are as cagey as a fox.

James Barry

Great, thanks. Nice to meet you James, that's a beautiful name. Firstly, may I ask how are you today?

Fine

Here are the details you requested...
Full name: Steven Elizabeth Higgins
Sex: Male
Age: 35
Country: United Kingdom of Great Britain and Wales
State: Happy
Your picture: Attached
Occupation: Mechanic
Monthly income: £3,400
Your purpose of joining the illuminati: I am interested in killing/sacrificing celebrities

Are you really interested to join the illuminati

Yes ma'am!

Ok, send me your pic now.

What sort of photo would you like? Clothed? Naked? Just my head/facial area?

Send me one of your picture

WOW! Are all Illuminati members so rude and abrupt??? Here you go, it's from my holiday in Spain in 2017. My hair is a bit longer now and a whole lot more greyer LOL (laughing online).

Ok

No LOL also? Mr Barry McGrump Pants!

Notice

1. Don't let anybody no that you are a member of illuminati or the freemason

2. You will meet the top people in the world and also work with them

3. If you are a member of illuminati, there is know going back

4. Even if you are a member, you can still live your normal life

5. Welcome to the place we're every body want to be

> Sorry, there are a few typos there, do you need some help?

No. Now you have to repeat this with a voice note record.
I receive the Illuminati as my life, my mentor, my hope.
I shall keep the secret to my self, no body shall no about it.
I remain to be an Illuminati till I die, I shall make money upon still I die, and if go back my gods of Illuminati kill me.
Now take this oath and send it back....ok

> That text you sent doesn't make sense. Can I change it so that it's better English?

Ok

> Thanks.

I SENT AN AUDIO NOTE OF ME READING HIS SCRIPT. I STUMBLED OVER WORDS, LAUGHED AND GENERALLY DID A PRETTY POOR JOB OF IT. BARRY THEN SENT ME A VIDEO OF A MAN CALLED DANIEL TURNER READING ONE OF THE BAD ILLUMINATI SCRIPTS. I'M NOT SURE WHY HE SENT IT TO ME, BUT I'M PRETTY SURE THE GUY IN THE VIDEO WAS ALSO TRYING TO WASTE THIS SCAMMER'S TIME.

> Who is Daniel Turner?!?! Did you send that by mistake?

Yes is one of us

Why did you send it to me? I thought you said we have to keep it secret? Why are you exposing Daniel Turner?

Is because you are now one of us

Oh cool, thanks. That was easy. Nice talking with you and thanks very much for your help. Have a good day x

You are not yet done with us first you have to do your initiation

Oh, so I'm not one of you yet? Then you shouldn't have told me about Daniel

Are you ready for the initiation now?

Yes ma'am

Ok, so how can you get the money to buy items for us to be able to initiate you? I promise two days after your initiation your riches famous and powerful you have already will be establish by the gram master him self and the donation money will be giving to you for you to start up a business

What items? You haven't mentioned any items, also GRAM master, haha! Do you mean GRAND Master??

Day are the items for your initiation to become a full member of the great illuminati

Day? Oh you mean THEY? Haha!

Thank for the correction

You're welcome ma'am. Please can you send me the details of the initiation process?

To all | Forward | Print | Delete | Show original
The items that will be used for your initiation will cost you $2,000 and after paying the fee you will be link up with someone in your country who will do your initiation for you to become a full member of the great Illuminati and in the day of you initiation some amount of money will be given to you and a new car for you to start your own life and you will also link up with some top people in your country and also outside your country just try and do it okay and become a full member of the Illuminati.

What does forward print delete show mean? Sorry I don't understand. Your message is very badly written. $2,000 is fine, but I don't want a new car. I just want to be able to kill celebrities.

A car is what we have. But what will give is power fame riches it will be up to you what to do with them after your initiation

God I'm excited! What do I do to get things started?

We see with one eye we don't talk much

What are you talking about??? I asked what I need to do to start the initiation.

Examples... Let me volk some spirit right away to confirm if your initiation will granted

Volk? That's not a real word. What do you mean?

Dead but still leaving, never been a real word

Volk means dead but still living? What are you talking about? Why are you telling me this?

I am only saying you that to know what you want to involve your self with

I'll ask again... what do I need to do to start the initiation?

You have to first take an oath with me

                                                    Right

That you are not hear to take our real
deep secret to the world

                                        Not HERE you mean?

Let like I said dead but still leaving, nothing is real

                            WHAT? You're not making sense! What
                            do I need to do to start the initiation?

Follow instructions

                                Give me some instructions then!

Oath I said

                                    Yes, I read about the oath...

You record the oath on your voice for
the confirmation of your initiation

                            OK, but you need to give me the oath!

⛰ THE ILLUMINATI ⛰
Aspirating Illuminati membership oath.

You are to make an AUDIO record of the 7-oath statements below
The AUDIO of your oath shall be submitted in our temple in the gathering of the great twelve heads (great world leaders) and played before the twelve heads and the great lord for approval. Try as much as you can to be loud while taking your oath.
We hope to hear from you as soon as possible

🔺 OATH 🔺

i. I will guide the course of the Illuminati with my heart

ii. I will keep the secrets of illuminati personal 🔺

iii. I will be my brother's keeper 🔺
iv. I will be ready to perform the necessary initiation ritual 🔺

v. A year after my membership I will bring a minimum of three members into the illuminati. 🔺

vi. I will never undo this step I have taken today 🔺

vii. If I fail to comply with the terms I have taken ,may it cost me the wealth fame and power I received 🔺

Regards 🔺
Thaddeus Iam

Who is Thaddeus Iam?

That is grand master

Rang dang diggedy dang di-dang!

I hope that is ok sub master. It's difficult to hold down the record button with blood on my fingers.

That is the oath dear

Thank you my love. That was fun, what is the next step please sir?

Dear Brother, thanks you for agreeing to Illuminati Terms and Conditions. We are glad you are ready to become a Faithful Servant to lucifer

Lucifer? The Devil??? You really should have mentioned you're a Satanic organisation before you gave me the oath! You worship the Devil?

Illuminati is what they call the 666

So you worship the Devil?

Forget about those talk

No, it's important. I need to know. You said this is important.

After your initiation you will understand
and know what I mean

Yes ma'am

Next step, you will send the item
money to mother licifer

Who is mother licifer?

For the preparation of your you initiation.

But who is mother licifer?

The only woman among men that is
more than the word that we get
initiation items for. You can as well
recall the oath you took, you will know
everything you need to know in the
temple.

Where is the temple? Is there one near me?

Every body is around you, dead but still living

OK good, because I won't be able to
go there for some time as I am
currently in prison for murder.

Hang on! What?? Dead but still living?
Do you mean ghosts? Because I don't
believe in ghosts.

What is ghost, it a greeting to a brother hood

Right...

Like I told you will know everything
from the grand master at the temple.
Next step

Yes, next step. Hit me with it, brother!

You will send the money for the item to
the mother lucifer for your item

Ohhh, mother lucifer.... you said licifer
before. OK, how do I send it?
Also, I can't go to the temple, I am in
prison.

There are temple every where even
inside the prison

Oh OK.... it must be well hidden. So
how do I send the money my lord?

Through western union or western
union money tranfer or to her direct
account

It'll have to be direct.... we don't have a
Western Union Money Gram station in
the prison. Wester Union is mostly used
by criminals and fraudsters... imagine if
they had one in the prisons!! HAHA!

The prison would be as all those scum in Nigeria who scam people!

Focus piz

Can you let me know the direct account details then please, sir?

Here
Account Name: CADRANE JOSH
Account Number: 84-308-376
Bank Name: ZIRAAT BANK
IBAN:
TR36-0001-0026-4684-3083-7650-02
Bank Address: 2646-RADAR-YENIBOSNA-branch, istanbul Turkey
Swift Code: TCZBTR2AX

When you are through sending the money give me an immediate alert, and are you sending now?

I should be able to go to the library at 4pm o'clock British London time and I have access to a full computing system there which is capable of performing complex banking transactions.

Like I said are you sending right away?

Well, no. Like I said, idiot, it'll be at 4pm o'clock British London time. That's 90 minutes time. Who is Cadrane Josh?

The woman that sells the items we are
getting for your initiation

OK great, she sounds nice. I heard the
Illuminati were responsible for Justin
Bieber's murder. Is that true?

Dear enough

Huh, we cannot talk?

Not yet till after your initiation.

Hmmmm you seem rude. I'm not sure I
want to go ahead if people in the
Illuminati are like you. I think I've
changed my mind, you seemed friendly
to start with.

I told you after your initiation you will
know and see every thing for your self

Candy Farmer went "stern Norman"
when the bobbies copped the look on
his Cleveland banger!

You said in 90 minutes right

It is less than 90 minutes now, time has
progressed in your favour. It is now
only 73 minutes.

72 minutes

I can't wait to get out of my cell!

After you have payed that to the
mother Lucifer you can as well then ask
any thing.

The first thing I'm going to do, after I
pay Master Cadrane Josh, is rip a new
chin hole in Martin Dunlop.

And your initiation will comment immediatel

So Master Cadrane Josh is mother Lucifer?

Yes

But I am in prison, how will you initiate
me here? I only get of my cell for four
hours a day

How many time will I tell you.

I don't know. Six? How many times
would you like to tell me?

Until you are initiated you will know
everything always

67 minutes

So after I am initiated I will know nothing? But before then I will know everything?

65 minutes

64 minutes

63 minutes

I am so excited to get out of my cell. Warden said if I am well behaved he'll let me buff his shoes.

62 minutes

Do you know, a conferternity called boddies, monk, hiddus, they are all under us

No, I don't know what you mean

They are secret court

I don't know what a conferternity is. And boddies and monk? A monk is a person, a singular person.

But they are nothing without us

I think you're confused, a monk is a MAN! Do you means monkS in general? All monks? You mean monasteries?

60 minutes

After your inititiation you will confirm all

Why say then?!?!?! You keep giving me stupid facts that don't make sense and when I try to clarify your stupidity you don't have an answer

Remaining 60 to send the money right?

No, 59 minutes, idiot

58 minutes

Hello let me tell you something it like you don't understand what I am telling you

I don't understand because you don't make sense. You need to try to make more sense man, you talk like a special needs child form the 80s.

57 minutes

Those are secret courts under the illuminati we are the greatest on the planet

A monk is a man, not a secret court!

The night

55 minutes

Boddies

Good, boddies... clever boy

Hiddus

54 minutes

I still don't know what you are talking about though.

53 minutes

When are you sending they money now?

51 minutes

50 minutes

That minute went quick.

Boy oh hecking flip wasp! I can't wait to be all powerful!

You will be initiated inside there and move out immediately power in the highest level

47 minutes

46 minutes

Ooooh yeah, I can feel the freedom, I can almost taste the blood of the innocent.

45 minutes

Beef me, major!

Tick tock, tick tock.... 43 minutes

Well paint me orange and call me Trump!

34 minutes my lord

32 minutes submaster

Oh no! I did the mathematics wrong. 22 minutes! Even closer to my destiny

21 minutes

Can I get a whoop whoop!?? 🎉🎉🎉🎉🎉🎉

Are you excited, James?

Once the woman confirm your payment
I will congratulate you

Blow my ass, it's so close now! Merely
18 Earth minutes away.

Make your payment and see this next
activation immediately

See this next activation immediately??
What does that mean?

17 minutes

Is seeing this next activation
immediately important? Because I
don't understand what you mean.

Enough till your payment is made.

Should I delay the payment and
research this phrase? I don't want to
pay if I don't know what "see this next

activation immediately" means. Please can you explain.

What is an activation and how do I see it? QUICK, we only have 15 minutes

Activation means the power that will be around you.

Ohhhh, OK. So you means once I have paid I will see this new activation around me immediately. Sorry, your English is VERY bad, you speak like a full spastic.

14 minutes

Because after you payment that means your are ready for initition

Yes I understand now, it's just your English is bad, you speak like a first year muffler on groodle.

13 minutes

Initiation

Correct ✅

When I am a member I will help you with your spelling and grammar, you will be able to recruit even more people once you can type properly.

12 minutes

I am not a computer list

What is a computer list?

11 minutes

You are not here for that

Brothers can't help brother in the Illuminati? You REALLY need help, almost everything you have said to me hasn't made sense.

Ok dear

Your spelling is bad, you use the wrong words, the wrong grammar. You don't seem to actually understand what you are saying.

So I would LIKE to help you as a thank you

9 minutes

With my help you could recruit many many more member

After everything you will teach me agreed

You could recruit richer and more intelligent members like Lord Douglas Howley, the millionaire, I have his contact details but he wouldn't speak to you at the moment the way you type.

8 minutes

Time for prayer to my grand master

Yes, I will pray for him too. I will pray he gets wealth, hot chicks and free bread.

What your problem, control your self dear

My problem is I am in prison and I want power. You will help me. The Illuminati will help me.

Power you will get

I have riches already but I want freedom and power!

Make you payment and start getting your power

Yes ma'am. In just 6 minutes time.

I want to lick the frosting off of cakes and put the boring bit back. I want bumper stickers with humours quotes. I want a cat that can talk and 40 copies of the Harry Potter series on Blu-Ray.

5 minutes

Oh they are early!!! They have come to let me out! I will go to the library and pay on the computer system there. ZERO minutes!

Ok

They won't let me leave the cell 😭 I told them I needed to pay the man from the Illuminati and they said I am suffering for psychotic delusions and that you are not real. I need to prove to them that you are real!

I don't get you

They say I'm crazy. My computum privileges have been permanently revoked. I cannot pay you the cash monies required. I'm so sorry my sexy lord.

Know?

Know, I am not allowed.

You have put the life of your son and
your self at risk

I don't have a son!

You want to know what we can do,
when you took an aoth

Please my lord, the oath was mistake.

Do you think you will live to see the next 7 days?

Please sir, what are you going to do to
me here in prison?

Kill you and your family

You don't even know my real name.

Until that seventh day

OK, do you need my address or something then?

BLOCKED.

The Illuminati Shopping List

ONCE AGAIN THE ILLUMINATI HAVE INVITED ME TO PREPARE FOR AN INITIATION CEREMONY, BUT IN ORDER TO GET THINGS MOVING I HAD TO BUY SOME SPECIAL ITEMS.

I SPOKE TO AN ILLUMINATI RECRUITMENT AGENT NAMED JAMES WHITE. HE FIRST GOT IN TOUCH BY LEAVING A COMMENT ON MY WEBSITE, IT INCLUDED A PHONE NUMBERS, SO I SENT HIM A MESSAGE ON WHATSAPP AND WASTED ABOUT SIX HOURS OF HIS LIFE, TIME HE COULD HAVE SPENT SCAMMING OTHER PEOPLE. HIS ORIGINAL MESSAGE SAID:

JOINING THE ILLUMINATI BRINGS YOU INTO THE LIMELIGHT OF THE WORLD IN WHICH YOU LIVE IN TODAY. YOUR FINANCIAL DIFFICULTIES ARE BROUGHT TO AN END. CALL: +2349067123738

We support you both spiritually , financially, physically and materially to ensure you live a comfortable life. It does not matter which part of the world you live in . From the united states down to the most remote part of the earth, we bring you all you want. Being an illiterate or a literate is not a barrier to being a millionaire between today and the next two weeks. You being in this our official website today signifies that it was ordered and arranged by the great lucifer that from now on, you are about to be that real and independent human you have always wished you were. We don't discriminate if you are white or black.

WhatsApp: +2349067123738 or WhatsApp me on +2349067123738 or send an email to illuminatytemple0@gmail.com for the next up coming initiation.

Hello, is this the Illuminate please?

Yes, how many are help you

You posted on my cat blog about joining your prestigious organisation. I don't know if I am worthy but I would like to apply please.

How do you get my count

Count?

I'm asking you

Yes, but what does count mean?

I said that do you counting me for help

What???? Why do you keep talking about counting?? What are you trying to say?

Do you really ready to join us here

I don't know, it depends what's involved. I've always wanted to join but I don't know anything about the Illuminati because it is secret.

Ok. No human and no women blood sacrifice

The Illuminati does sacrifice humans!

No human no women blood sacrifice

Yes, the illuminati sacrifice celebrities.

How

Everyone know the Illuminati killed Prince, Michael Jackson, John Lennon, John F. Kennedy, Agatha Christie, Martin Luther King, Jr., and many many more...

My main reason for joining is because I want to help sacrifice celebrities

No it because of their disobedience

But still they were killed. Therefore the Illuminati IS an organisation that kills.

Yes

So why did you say they didn't?

That is why I don't want you to know that it

Why? Everyone knows that.

What is your name. I old are you

Well, why don't you introduce yourself first, that would be polite? My name is Steve Higgins and I am 35 years of oldness.

What is your occupation

I asked you to introduce yourself

We're are you chat from

I'm not going to give all my details to a stranger. What is your name?

My name is James White

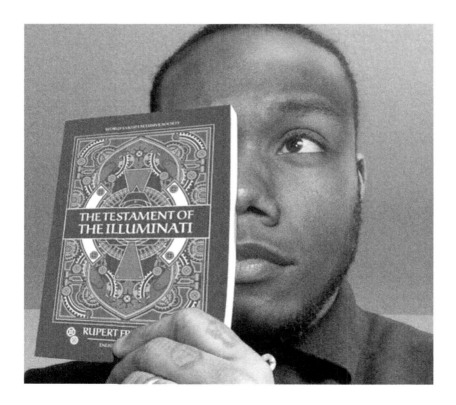

Oh, I know him! That's Chad Tiecheck. Why have you sent me a photo of Chad? I have that book too. Shall I take a photo of me with it?

Yee

Have you read it? It's pretty funny isn't it. I wasn't sure if a real Illuminate member would find it funny or not though?

It ain't funny bruv

It is, it's a comedy book. A spoof book, that's not a REAL Illuminati book.

Hahaha

No, seriously. It's a spoof book. It's available on Amazon. It is very funny. Anyway, can you help me?

Yes I can that's why I'm here

Where are you from James?

I'm Nigerian

That makes sense because the Illuminati are all very wealthy. Nigeria is a rich country?

All you need to do now you are to fill in the form first immediately okay

OK, my darling

We're are you chat from

Bedfordshill

MEMBERSHIP FORM
So you want to become a great member of the Illuminati kingdom you have to fill the real Illuminati form and get back to us immediately.
SURNAME:_____
NAME:_____
GENDER:_____
AGE:_____
COUNTRY:_____

STATE:_____
CITY:_____
PARENTS NAMES:_____
PROFESSION:_____
OCCUPATION:_____
SKILLS/TALENTS/SKILLS:_____
MARITAL STATUS:_____
SPOKEN LANGUAGE:_____
PHONE NUMBER:_____
MONTHLY INCOME_____
REASON FOR JOINING:_____
Regards,
GRAND MASTER

Oh I hate forms

I you really ready to fill in the form

What?

You are not my question

What? You're not making sense

SURNAME: Higgins
NAME: Steve
GENDER: Greckterphobe
AGE: 35
COUNTRY: United Kingdom of Great
Britain and Wales
STATE: Happy
CITY: London
PARENTS NAMES: Gary and Simon
PROFESSION: None
OCCUPATION: None

SKILLS/TALENTS/SKILLS: What? Why is skills here twice?
MARITAL STATUS: Married, one kid, but that didn't work out so I married an adult.
SPOKEN LANGUAGE: English
PHONE NUMBER: You have it
MONTHLY INCOME: I don't work
REASON FOR JOINING: I want to kill/sacrifice celebrities

Ok

So, how do we get started?

The Illuminati is an elite organization of world leaders, business authorities, and other influential members of this planet. Our collective unites influencers of the world in an unrestrictive and private domain, free of political, religious, and geographical boundaries to further the prosperity of the human species as a whole.

Right

Have u go true it

True?

Ok

Illuminati the abundance of valuable
resources or valuable material
possessions. This includes:
Long-term prosperity. Be extradinary
from the rest.
Fame - Join us and become
internationally recognized.
Power - Illuminati is one of the most
powerful families.
Money - Join us today and kick out
your financial problems.

Are you internationally recognised then?

Make sure you are going true it okay

What do you mean by true? I am
always honest if that's what you mean.

Not really just want to know

OK, well everything I have said is true

OK

I want you to trust me and take my
words so that you can achieve your
dreams of becoming a millionaire and
billionaire okay... I will do everything
possible for you to be a member of the
great Illuminati organization okay

Millionaire AND billionaire? That would
be like a billion-millionaire!

You'll have to send us a scanned or attached copy of your identity card so that we will have an idea of the person we are dealing with considering the above conditions of this organization, if they are acceptable to you, you are advice to give me a quick response.

OK, I am just on my way home. I will take the photo of my driving license when I am there in about 7 minutes

Okay, be fast so we can go folder

Folder? What do you mean?

I mean u should be fast to send it

Oh, why did you say FOLDER then?

It was the key board mistake are u sending it

I already have, idiot

Okay

TERMS AND CONDITION OF THE ILLUMINATI

In accordance to the supreme leader of the elite. You are expected to agree to the following
1. Keep our relationship a secret
2. Pay your regular dues every year
3. Help other members in any way you can
4. Fight to keep the society in peace and order
5. Go through all the process of joining the elite
6. Obey our rules and regulations

If you agree to the above. You are advise to say a YES or NO so as to know if we can proceed. NOTE that you are not force to join us it is on your decision

Signed by: MR JAMES
(initiation agent)
Kingsleekwebelem

> That is mostly fine but I have a couple of questions. It says signed Mr James.... your name is Mr White isn't it?

That's the name of the grand master PA

> And what does Kingsleekwebelem mean? Sorry, I'm new to all of this.

That's the place where ur initiation we be don

> What? That's not a place?!?

That's the name of the house

Where is it?

At california

Oh OK great, that's not too far from me. I'll look it up on the Google Mapping system and see. What are the regular dues?

To re-new ur initiation

So how frequent are these payments and how much are they?

I need to earn your trust..without trust we can't go far. I want to let you know that I have helped a lot of people and I know you won't be the last

OK, but still I need to know these details. I might not be able to afford to make the regular payments.

Know

Know what? What do I know?

To be a full member of the Illuminati, you are to get some items which will beside for your initiation

Yes, but I need to know about these regular dues. Please can you explain, I don't know if I'll be able to afford it.

Okay, i want you to know the initiation items which will be use to initiate you

Wait! I want to know about the regular dues. There's no point carrying on if I can't afford the regular dues. I need to know how much I have to pay and how often.

The regular dues is like a firm if offering to lord baphoment

No, regular dues means regular payments. Don't you understand your own rules?

Pay your dues regularly that is the law not regular due

Yes.... I NEED to know how much the dues are and how regularly. Are you new?

Do you even know the amount of the dues

That's what I'm asking!!!!! I've asked about twenty times how much the dues are and how often I have to pay.

100$

$100. OK, good. How often?

Any time you go to the temple

No, that wouldn't be what REGULAR means. Go away and check.

Don't understand

I want you to check with your masters how often the REGULAR $100 needs to be paid. REGULAR DUES are paid usually either yearly, monthly, weekly. I need to know how often I have to pay $100.

OK let me ask him

Thank you

OK, the grand master seld that is muothly

Monthly? OK great thanks, so you are not a member then?

Who told you that

Well you obviously don't pay regular dues and that is rule number two. Even the GRAND MASTER IS WRONG!!! I've just noticed, the rules say "2. Pay your regular dues every year" YEARLY! Not monthly!

Are u trying to say am not real agent or what

Well, explain to me why YOU didn't know it was yearly. It says YEARLY in the rules YOU sent me, I just didn't notice but you should KNOW.

Not yearly OK are you to tell me the rules

YOU said yearly! Not me. I know the rules better than you. You didn't even know what REGULAR DUES meant, let alone how often they had to be paid and when you asked your grand master he GOT IT WRONG

It's a mistake from key board I told you before

So is it monthly or yearly?

Monthly I seld

Yes you did say but you also said that REGULAR meant you pay it whenever you go to the temple... which is COMPLETELY WRONG. So I need to check in case you make any more mistakes.

$100 a month is fine. So, what's next?

For you to join the great Illuminati you will have to be initiated and for your initiation to take place there are some certain items you Will need to purchase :
1 Edin
2 Ogirigon
3 Illuminati Saint
4 Illuminati Oil
5 Mustard Seed
6 A lamb
7. A big Native Goat to replace human Blood
8. Trunk
9. White cowries
10. Native chalk
11. Eboriwo
12. Red kola with five face
13. Eagle's Heart to represent bravery
All together is $4500

$4500 is fine for the initiation, that's not too much.

Know not much

Know what? You don't know much? Or I don't know much?

I said it's not much

No, it's not

Can you get the items

Yeah, that shouldn't be a problem. There's an occult store near me and three of my friends are in the Illuminate. When do I need it by?

Can u get them all

Yeah, I don't see why not. A lamb and goat, easy... my family run a farm.

Edin, ogriigon, eboriwo and trunk I should be able to get from the occult store, it's only about two miles away.

Illuminati Saint and oil, I don't know what that is but my friends can get that for me.

Mustard seed, native chalk and white cowries are obviously easy to get, just in the supermarket.

Y did u not tell ur friend to initiate u

Well because you are not allowed to invite a friend or family member, they must get in on their own merit. You should know this.

Who told u that

I can't tell you his name obviously. Sorry, I know I'm not supposed to know but he told me when he was drunk. It seems like I know more about the rules than you!

U are lieing right

What? That's what my friend said

Send me ur friend number

No, he'll get in trouble for telling me the secrets

Am a member right so u can not tell me my rules okay

No, you should know I can't tell that

U are not really

Anyway, forget that sir, when do I need these items by?

By tomorrow

OK that's fine

How are you going to get it

Well, like I said, it's all pretty easy to get. I just asked my friend about Illuminati Saint and oil…

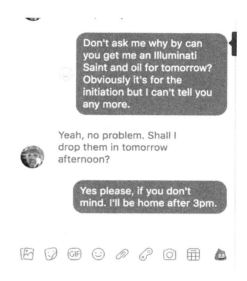

Don't ask me why by can you get me an Illuminati Saint and oil for tomorrow? Obviously it's for the initiation but I can't tell you any more.

Yeah, no problem. Shall I drop them in tomorrow afternoon?

Yes please, if you don't mind. I'll be home after 3pm.

Which supermarket

Walmart's super store

If u can get them let me now so I call someone to get them for me an bring it to our temple

Oh it should be fine. Mustard seed is pretty cheap.

Can u send the money to the person so them can get it for u

It would be quicker if I went and got it myself tonight.

What u are sending is not even what we need here

Yes it is, mustard seed are mustard seeds. How can mustard seed be anything else? There's a whole page of different types, shall I just buy one of each? I'm going to go to Walmart now. I should have everything within 24 hours. Please can you tell me the address of the temple, I couldn't find Kingsleekwebelem on Google Maps.

I u not take it seriously we will not proceed with the initiation

Oh, please! I bought mustard seeds already.

No, u are not dedicated to the cause

OK, but one last question before you go… do you know any nice Nigerian recipes that include mustard seed?

Resting Grinch Face

WHAT DO YOU DO DURING THOSE QUIET FEW DAYS OVER THE FESTIVE PERIOD, THAT WEIRD GAP BETWEEN CHRISTMAS AND THE NEW YEAR? WASTE THE TIME OF A SCAMMER OF COURSE!

Hey how you doing?

Not bad thanks, how about you?
Excited for Christmas?

I'm good. What's your name and there
are you from?

I'm Steve, I'm from the small rural
village of England. How about you?

I'm Bella from Maryland. Tell me about yourself.

I work in a ballet school for children
with oddly shaped feet.

I'm single funny I'm not working at this
moment I lost my job when my dad
passed away

I'm pleased to hear about your loss

What are you doing now?

I'm at home at the moment, just polishing my uncles. Are you working today?

No I'm not

What do you do?

I work in the coffee shop

Hang on, I thought you said you lost your job?

I work in the coffee shop earlier

So are you job hunting at the moment?

Yes already I hope I get one sooner

What sort of thing are you looking for?

I don't know like to be a delivery lady, work In a restaurant or a waiter in a coffee just like before

That should be easy enough to find then shouldn't it? The service industries are always crying out for slower, unskilled workers.

I hope it will be easy. How does your work goes?

We just help the kids by re-moulding their feet in a dance setting sometimes we used dangerous exotic animals as encouragement.

What do you like to do in your free time?

I like touching various objects, walking in the countryside and watching adult movies, but sometimes that causes me to trip over stray logs and branches.

Ohhh, I see. I hope you wouldn't ask me for my nudes picture as every other guys I've met always do.

No, I hate nude women, they make me sick. That's why I trip over so much, I generally keep my eyes closed while watching my specialist movies.

Ok good

What do you like to do in your time that is spare?

I like to walk around the beach, I love sports, I listening to different kind of musics, dancing, singing, I love adventures, traveling, outdoor festivals, swimming, and movies.

Where in Maryland do you live? Near the coast?

Yes

Where in Maryland?

East coast sorry for the late response I went to pee

That's OK, I just had a quick dump while I was waiting. Maryland is on the east coast, I mean which city?

Parkville, Burridge road

Oh, near Baltimore. So you're quite a long way from the beach then?

I spend the day if I do go there

Oh nice, which beach do you go to? I've seen some amazing beaches in Maryland.

Miami Beach park.

Miami? Miami in Florida?

Yes Miami

That's 1,000 miles from Maryland. You go there for the day???

It public beach in Maryland here it name Miami beach park. Not the real Miami.

Ohhhhh, right. That makes more sense. Still quite a long way, what 70 miles?

Yes that why I stay there for days I go there for my vacation

Have you ever been to the UK?

I am originally from Milton Keynes uk

Oh cool, the ostrich capital of the world!

Yea

When did you move to the US?

About 3 years now because I lost my dad and I've being wanting to change my environment

So your coffee shop job was in the UK then?

No I work in the coffee shop here earlier not in Milton Keynes I wasn't working then my dad was alive

You said you lost your job when your dad died

Hell I was a model then but I was
working from home then not in a coffee
shop

Heck! So you were a model in the UK?

Not anymore because I haven't
complete the course study for it so I
quit

Haha study to be a model, good one!

A professional one not just a local one

Yeah, it's not really something you can
study though is it?

I was study online back in Milton
Keynes but I'm not anymore, you got to
go for it course and get a certificate for
it

A modelling certificate?!?!?! You're
pulling my chunkers!

Look I got to learn about it so that I can
know what and what they do and how
they do things

But you were already a model before,
did you certificate lapse?

I haven't being hired yet

This is getting confusing. You literally told me you were working as a model in the UK but you lost your job when your dad died. Now you are saying you were never hired. Which job did you lose when your dad parked his chops?

I lose the course because I can't afford the tutor again

If you want to be a model though, just do it, you don't need a certificate!

Look I wanna do some other work for a bit before I start my future career

Doing what?

I wanna get a job

Yeah, what sort of job? Butcher? Baker? Candlestick maker?

I don't know whatever one I see

Hang on, you said earlier you did know what type of work you wanted. You said something in the service industry or delivery driver.

Whatever one that come first

                You keep saying different and conflicting things

Yes look whatever one I see you
disturbing my brain talk about
something else

                Sorry, I didn't realise it was a sensitive
                subject. You said you like festivals, me
                too. Have you been to any of the big
                ones in Maryland?

Yes

                            Which ones?

I can't remember

                You can't remember? You asked me to
                choose a topic and now you're
                avoiding it.

What your plans for the rest of the day?

                Nothing, I'm just staying in touching up
                my book ends and furnishing teets. It's
                very cold. Is it hot there still?

Yes

Really? The unusual for Maryland in the winter.

Yes it sunny here now

The weather website says it's 2°C

Okk I be going to shop to get get
something to eat now I talk to you
when I get home

OK, have a good time. Wrap up warm...
or cool! Hahah, who knows?!?

Hmm

A LITTLE LATER, BUT LONG ENOUGH TO FORGET THE LIE...

Hi

Did you enjoy your trip to the shop?

Shop?

You said you were going to the shop to
get something to eat

I get some chips

Oh nice

What you doing now?

Just having a bit of Branston on segments before bed

Ok

I bet you miss Branston out there.
What else do you miss from England?

Weather

Which British show is your favourite? I
love Jet Wash! Do you remember the
one where Bobby Trisps got lost at sea
and came back all red and sun burnt!
HAHA!

Yesssss lol

Haha! Yeah, classic! Two weeks in a
dingy! I always say Bobby's
catchphrase when I talk to people at
work.... "do I look crispy?! It's Trisps,
with a T!"

Ok

Good, I'm glad that's ok

What your plans for tomorrow?

Well, Christmas Eve tomorrow, so the usual. I think the burning starts around here at about 6 o'clock. It's a really good one this year, all the figures are made out of straw so it's much greener. Do they do the nativity burn in the US as well?

Yes sure

Really? That's surprising, how does it work there because obviously they drive on the right

I don't understand

You know the nativity burn that we do here?

Yes

You said they do it in the US too, but because the stable faces east wouldn't it be facing the wrong way because they would be driving the precession on the right of the road.

I don't drive tho so I don't know much about it

What? No.

You wouldn't need to drive to know that.

I guess you haven't been to a nativity burn since you moved there?

Omg slow with your chat too much for me

Sorry, I'll slow down, I forgot you are quite stupid. I just enjoy chatting to you.

You typing so fast how come?

I just have a very fast brain. The doctor told me my brain works four times faster than normal humans.

Oh super what your plans for Christmas?

Christmas will be the usual, about 4,000 maggots and a vat of freezing cold water.

It gonna be bored with me because I live alone

You must be rich! How do you afford to live in Baltimore in your own place?

No I'm not rich

But it's an expensive city and you haven't had a job for three years

I got a uncle who live in Germany he
buy and sells article so he pay for me
for helping him for that

Oh great, it's good you have someone to support you

He's stop because I don't have anyone
to help me receive package again

Package?

Yes will you calm down and listen if I explain?

I am calm

He buy and sells article he get all the
items shipped to uk then the pick up
man will come pick it up from whoever
receive it to see it to the final
destination. He post a lot of articles
online so if anyone want them they will
request for it and he will ship it to uk
and from there the pickup man will
come pick it and get it deliver it to the
bloke who order for it do. You
understand now?

Yeah, he runs an eCommerce business

But now my friend who always help me
receive those package in uk already got
married so she said she won't have
time to sort out the parcels again. So
I'm now looking for a trustworthy

Person who will be helping me receive Package now. He's already loses loads of customer because I haven't help him get a deliver address in England

I don't really understand to be honest, but I hope he gets it sorted out, things are tough at the moment

Would you like to help me be receiving the package? and it gonna be picked up from you every week or you still don't understand?

So your uncle sends me a package from Germany. A Parcelforce driver picks it up from me, so how does it get to you?

It doesn't have to come to me again it get deliver straight away after picking it from you

So how do you help?

By helping him find a deliver address of who I trusted or better still my boyfriend

Why doesn't he just send it straight to the final destination?

It cost him a lot of money by that sometime package get missing if he send it straight

It should be cheaper because he wouldn't then need two couriers in the UK. At the moment he's paying international shipping and then a local courier, that's just stupid - family trait?

So he send it by Dhl Germany post and get it deliver to whoever in uk by parcelforce

Makes perfect sense! How many parcels would be delivered to me per month and how much would I get paid for each parcel?

It might be 15-20 parcels every two weeks would you let's do with 150 a month?

Yeah, that could work if everything checks out ok

Send me your address so I can see where you live

We can sort that tomorrow, it's getting late here

Ok dream about me

More like a nightmare, haha!

Good night!

DECEMBER 24 - CHRISTMAS EVE

Hi how did you sleep?

Hello, I slept on my side, thanks.

How are you feeling now?

My arm is a little numb, but other than that I am OK

Oh sorry

It's not your fault, the mattress was quite rigid, don't worry.

What your plans for today?

Well the nativity burn is at 6 o'clock. My father is the chief usher in this year's parade.

Really?

Yeah, during the pandemic he's helped a lot of the cats in the neighbourhood, so it's sort of a thank you for all his efforts. So, he'll get to ride at the front today with the Mexican hat on.

Oh ok

Are you going to go to the one near you?

No I'm not going I be home

Alone on Christmas eve? What a loser!

Yes

Oh that's sad. I wish I was there to keep you company

Ok

OK?

Yes

OK

LATER, AFTER THE NATIVITY BURN...

Hey

Hi, Kyle Isabella!

What you doing now?

Just watched the burn, it was brilliant apart from when the Mexican hat blew off my dad's head. God, I could have just eaten myself up with embarrassment. Now going to the pub with friends.

Ok

You should go to your local one, you might not be so bored. I guess they will start soon, what time does it get dark?

9pm

What? In the winter???

I just checked on Google, it gets dark at 5pm.

It 4:52pm here now

Yeah, so almost dark already!

Why did you say 9pm?

There?

No there.

Sunset in Maryland is 16:48

You said what time does it get dark here not what the current time here now

Yeah, it gets dark in Maryland at 5pm.

It's winter there.

Look send one message at a time, you
kill me with messages

Work out your story and tell me
tomorrow. I'm busy with friends. Good
night. I hope Santa brings you
something nice x

Smile

DECEMBER 25 - CHRISTMAS DAY

Good morning Steve

Merry Christmas!

What you doing now?

Opening the gifts the Lord Santa Christ
brought me

Ok

Merry Christmas!

Smile

You are up early. Excited to see what
Santa brought you?

I haven't get anything yet

Are you not going to wish me a merry Christmas? 😟

Merry Christmas 🎁🎄 Happy new year in advance

Thanks! 😃 That's made my day!

Really?

I didn't think you were going to say it. I thought you were mad at me.

No I am not mad at you

OK

When you are alone?

I told you already, you understand it's Christmas day?

What you mean?

It's Christmas day, you dappy cow! A time a family, celebration and casual sex. That's actually today. So I'm not likely to be alone.

Ok have you eaten?

Yeah, we had a traditional festive breakfast, have you?

What did you have?

Freshly baked chocolate sleeves

Ok

That's OK is it? Good

Yes

Just saying OK to everything is a bit dismissive. You don't sound every interested. You have no opinion on chocolate sleeves?

I don't want to get you distracted because you are with your family now

OK

Yes

Thanks

How would you describe me?

I would describe you as pretty but irritable, short tempered, slow, uninterested and quite stupid. How would you describe me?

Hun? 🙄

That's true. You are irritable and short tempered because you get angry and change the subject when I ask you a question. You are slow and stupid because you can't keep up with messages. And you are uninterested in me because you only ask short questions and when I answer you never want to know more, you just say "OK" every time. Plus you didn't even wish me a merry Christmas until I basically told you too. But you are every pretty and I would like to get to know you better.

Oh I'm sorry about my short messages and all that

That's OK. It's Christmas a time of forgiveness and platitude

Aww thanks for forgiving me

You're welcome, you stupid fool!

Guess your full now?

Full? No, why?

You had enough food

We had breakfast about two hours ago
and chocolate sleeves are only small

Ok

I'm glad that is OK

LATER ON CHRISTMAS DAY...

What you doing now?

Realigning the Christmas brushes

Okk you having fun now I guess

Well as much fun as you can have
aligning brushes! HAHAHAHA

Ok

I'm glad that is OK

LATER STILL ON CHRISTMAS DAY...

What you doing now?

Helping to un-cook the Christmas time dinner.

Okk what you cooking

The turkey has already been cooked,
I'm just helping to un-cook it now.

Ok

I'm glad that is OK

Yes

OK

VERY LATE ON CHRISTMAS DAY...

What are you doing now?

Just about to blush the Santa figurine

Ok

Is that OK?

Yes. I wanna ask you a question

Sure, ask away....

Do you want my uncle to be laying every two weeks or every month?

It's Christmas day I don't want to talk business now and you shouldn't be either. Go and enjoy yourself!

Oh my bad I'm sorry about that

It's OK, it makes me laugh like this "hahaha"

Ok

I'm glad it is OK

What your plans for tomorrow?

Boxing day so obviously more celebration and the traditional boxing ceremony

Ok then

OK?

Ok

Good, I'm glad it's OK

What you want to talk about now?

Nothing really

Ok write to me when you less busy then

I'm glad it is OK

Thanks for the care

Uhhh... OK

DECEMBER 26 - BOXING DAY

How are you doing?

Good thanks, how about you?

Good too what are you doing now?

I'm driving to Old Mexico, just stopped at the service station for a Red Melt and Double Buffer bar.

Okkk

I'm glad that is okkk

Yes

How about you?

I'm good

No, I mean what are you doing?

Nothing at the moment

Sounds fun, I want some!

What you wanna talk about now?

What music do you like?

I listen to Justin Bieber

Justin Bieber?!? Hahahahahahaha

What about you?

I like a Spooky G and the Horse, Steve Corpse, Dog Melody, Carson Beach, Samantha Toblerone.... That sort of thing. Anything with a sort of 15-42 ranko beat.

Oh ok

I'm glad that's OK

DECEMBER 27

Hey how are you doing?

Just woke up, why are you up so early again?

I can't sleep what about you

I'm awake. It's not early here, but it's 5am there. You are always awake so early. I guess you don't get much sleep.

Yes I don't sleep much

Haha like Corvuz the Milo

Smile

You remember him?

Yes

Wow, chatty today!

What you be doing today?

It's still morning. Nothing yet. How about you, what are your plans?

You home now?

No, still in Old Mexico

Ok

I'm glad that is OK

When you going to be ready for
business?

It would be best to talk business once
I'm back at work in the new year, but I
asked what you are doing today? Why
are you ignoring me?

Nothing if the whether is good ima
have a lil walk out.

LATER THAT DAY...

What you doing now?

I'm currently driving back to England,
just stopped at Watford Chin service
station.

Okk

I'm glad that is OK

LATER STILL...

What did you have for dinner?

I had Gregg's at the services. What's your favourite thing from Gregg's?

I don't have a favorite

Oh..... well that's a way to kill a conversation

No we can talk about another thing again

You just never talk about any topic I suggest. How can you not have a favourite in Gregg's? Everyone does!

Hmm I'm sorry

So what do you like from Gregg's?

Hmm 🌝 I love everything

Why are you avoiding such a simple question? I'm trying to have a bit of fun and talk to you. Tell me your top three things from Gregg's....

It because I'm not in the mood to talk about that

No, you're never in the mood to talk about anything I want to talk about. It's all "me, me, me, OK, OK, OK..." etc!

Do you smoke or drink alcohol?

I drink alcohol, I'd imagine smoking it is pretty dangerous as it's so flammable

What kind of alcohol do you fancy?

I'm fine at the moment, thanks. What is your favourite alcohol?

I don't drink alcohol

Oh typical. Can't answer that question either then. What's your favourite Domino's pizza topping?

I've never gone to dominion pizza here in Maryland here

OK great, so you won't even answer a question about a good old Dominion pizza.

I swear I've answered the question, I've never being there before

Yeah, but your answer was you don't have a favourite. How can you have

never had a Dominion pizza? That's like
saying you've never been to a Bruno's
Wine Bar.

If I did have a favorite I would have tell you

Well you wouldn't tell me what your
favourite at Gregg's is, you said you
weren't in the mood to talk about it

Smile

I'm not smiling, big sad face looking right at you

Hmm

Have you ever been down to Cornwall
when you lived here?

No we didn't go there

Devon?

Yes

Oh cool, I love Devon. Where did you go?

It being long I can't really remember
but I've being there before

Oh what a surprise. You can't answer.

I did answer

You didn't you avoided the question
again. Let's try to work out where you
went in Devon, was it near the coast?

Yes near the coast

A town? Village?

Town

Where did you stay? Hotel? Campsite?
Caravan? Prison?

Caravan

A static caravan, tourer or ornamental one?

You always wanting to know everything
about things

Of course I do, we're supposed to be
getting to know one another, it's how it
works, I want to know everything about
you

Really 😆

Yes, that's what needs to happen in any relationship

I like chatting with you

I like chatting with you too most of the time, apart from when you are evasive about trivial things

Do you ever want kids?

Not live ones, no. Do you?

Yes I do

OK

Are you mad about me wanting a kids?

Mad? Why would I be mad?

I'm just asking because you want a different thing and I want a different thing

People are different

Would you still want me as I want kids?

It depends really, would you still want me if we didn't have kids?

Yes I will you gonna adopt one then

I'd adopt a kid if it was like a hot 22-year-old Porto Rican girl

Oh ok

I could help her get her showered and dressed for work and that

Oh ok

I'm glad that is OK

Do you think I'm kind of lady you desire
pls be honest

I don't know yet. I barely know you. That's why I'm trying to get you to talk and open up, but sometimes it's like trying to tease gravel out of a carcus with just a clutter bomb

Do you want to have a relationship with me?

I don't know yet, we are still getting to know each other

Understandable

Anyway, I'm falling asleep now. So I need to say good night.

Ok goodnight sweet dreams about me 𝐳𝐙ᶻ 😴 😚

DECEMBER 28

Good morning Steve

Good morning, Kyle

I tried to dream about you, but all my dreams were about giving our adopted 22-year-old daughter a bath

Omg 😂

It would be great. I'd give her such a thorough cleaning 🧼🧽

Ok

I'm glad it is OK

What you doing now?

I'm on the beach

Bastards aren't they?!

Ok

Bastards though aren't they?

What

Seagulls are bastards aren't they?

Yes

Oh little miss chatty again today I see? You have nothing more to say about seagulls than "yes"?? I don't know why I bother trying to make conversations. You didn't even laugh. Cold. Uninterested.

Ok I will talk more open

Thanks! Finally. So, seagulls hey. Aren't they bastards?

It is bastard

Anything funny ever happened to you involving one?

No

Do you know anyone who has had a funny experience with a seagull?

What you doing now

Topic change alert! 🖼️

Smile 😊

🙁 I'm not smiling, I'm incredibly angry

Why?

Because you don't ever have an
opinion on things or have a
conversation. If I ask something you
change the subject or become evasive
like when I asked you about Gregg's
yesterday.

Ok what can I do to make you smile?

Answer my questions properly

I did answer the question I don't know
anyone who had experience with a
seagull

OK, who's your favourite Top Of The
Pops presenter of all time?

What

What don't you understand? Who is
your favourite presenter of Top Of The
Pops of all time?

I understand now... Justin Bieber

What? Justin Bieber has never
presented Top Of The Pops. He would
have been a baby!

Really?

Haha yeah, really! What are you talking about??

I thought you mean my fav artist

No PRESENTER of TOP OF THE POPS? It's like talking a brain dead duck.

Jenifer lopez is that what you mean

No, I don't get why you don't understand such a simple question. Your favourite host/presenter of Top Of The Pops

Ohh now I understand well I don't have a fav presenter host

Oh God! OK, which Top Of The Pops presenter DON'T you like?

I like all of them

Even Jimmy? How about this.... Just name any Top Of The Pops presenter just to give me something back and something to talk about

AFTER SOME TIME ON GOOGLE...

Noel Edmonds, Tommy Vance and Tony Dortie

Oh cool, so all the black ones then?

Yea

Hello what are you doing now?

Just sat having my afternoon movement

OK

I'm glad that is OK

What you want to talk about now?

There's no point me suggesting a topic, you don't answer. What do you want to talk about?

Anything you choose

Where did you go on family holidays when you were younger?

We travel to Kent sometimes ago then

Oh cool, unusual holiday destination. Where did you go in Kent?

Sheerness have you being there before?

Yeah, I've been there. They have that amazing underwater dental college and that house made out of golden ears.

Ok

I'm glad that is OK

Where have you been to again?

Loads of places, I went to Nuneaton last week

Okk you are interesting

Thanks, but I said... I went to Nuneaton last week

Really?

That was a joke. You were supposed to laugh. You have a terrible sense of humour!

I know what you talking about but I don't wanna say what gonna make you feel bad

Why would it make me feel bad? It's OK to laugh at jokes. You should laugh, it would make you less boring

I was about to say where is that fuck is

What?? You don't know Nuneaton!

No I don't

It's the nearest big city to Milton Keynes where you grew up!

I know I remembered my bad I nearly forgot

So now you get the joke?

Hmm look I don't really have much experience I'm pretty new to online stuff

So you only get jokes in real life, just not online? Here's one...

Why didn't Santa deliver any presents to the kids in Manchester this year?

How would I know when I'm not in uk now

Wasping hell! It was CLEARLY the set up for a joke! Santa isn't real!

Hmm

You don't understand jokes? Let's try again.... Why didn't Santa deliver any presents to the kids in Manchester this year?

Smile

No! You know how a joke works? Surely. The normal response is "I don't know".

Yes I know

OK, so let's try again....

Ok

Why didn't Santa deliver any presents to the kids in Manchester this year?

I don't know

Because he couldn't Oldham all!

Smile 😊

I love having you to chat to even though you're quite stupid and very annoying at times.

Smile ok

Smile back, I'm glad it is OK. It's good you don't mind me calling you stupid, it's important for me to be honest with you.

Why you call me stupid?

Because you don't understand things.

I need to go and make my nails now

Make your nails?

Yes

What does that mean?

Fix my fingernails

Fix them? They are broken?

No I wanna fix another one

Another what?

Another nails

Another nails? You're not making sense.

You don't understand again

I think you means "get my nails DONE". Not make or fix, you just speak in a really strange way, I think it's because you are so stupid.

Fuck enough bye

HAHAH! I win. The parcel forwarding scammer has finally had enough. I've had so much fun annoying you with all these questions for the last week, and what a massive waste of your time it has been, I've been laughing all week long. You really are VERY STUPID!

Your mom is stupid

Hahahahahahahahahahahaha

Printed in Great Britain
by Amazon

15068278R00132